Successful People Management In A Week

W9-AMC-017

Dr Norma Barry

The Teach Yourself series has been trusted around the world for over 60 years. This series of 'In A Week' business books is designed to help people at all levels and around the world to further their careers. Learn in a week, what the experts learn in a lifetime.

Norma Barry has four decades experience of working in managerial roles within the public sector from executive to director level. She has worked in a wide variety of policy areas and spent 15 years of her career working with businesses, including major energy and telecommunication companies, and food and drinks processing companies of all sizes. This experience gave her valuable insight into the private sector. Norma has a Ph.D. in Leadership and Change Management and an MBA from Cardiff Business School. She is passionate about leadership and management and has been an active volunteer within the Chartered Management Institute as well as with local business schools. Norma currently runs her own company, helping organizations identify their problems and put things right, in particular supporting them on managing change.

For more information, go to www.IOOS.co.uk

I have always been particularly interested in people management, primarily because during my career I experienced poor and ineffective management. However, I learned from these, sometimes painful, experiences which strengthened my resolve to continually learn about the practice of management through on-the-job experiences and reflection, supplemented by study and other development opportunities. People managers have considerable power to make a difference to others and the business of organizations. I hope that this book will help you become a good and respected people manager.

Teach Yourself®

Successful People Management

Dr Norma Barry

www.inaweek.co.uk

Contents

Introduction

This book, *Successful People Management In A Week*, is primarily for new or aspiring managers. It is also a useful reference tool for junior and middle managers who are looking to develop their skills and are, possibly, seeking progression in their careers. The book aims to give readers a sound understanding of the concept of people management; the role of people managers; people motivational theories; the various people management styles and their appropriateness; the tools available to people managers to help them do their jobs effectively; techniques for managing performance; and an insight into how people managers can develop their teams. It concludes with advice on how to survive as a people manager in tough times.

Each of the following chapters provides concise accounts of various aspects of people management for every day of the week. The reader is expected to spend between one and two hours each day studying the daily topic and checking his or her understanding against the specified learning goal.

At the end of the week, readers should have gained a full appreciation of:

The meaning of people management

The functions of a people manager at various levels in an organization

How to apply motivational theories to people management

The managerial tools that are available and the situations in which they can be used

The various people management styles and their benefits and drawbacks

Advice and tools for the development of teams

How to survive in tough times.

Management, along with leadership, is one of the most studied topics on organizations. There is a wealth of literature covering the subject and there are many views on what makes a good manager and their roles together with how effective teams are managed and developed. Many hold the view that management is best learned through doing. Nevertheless, this book provides practising, junior and aspiring managers with a fundamental understanding of the principles and challenges of managing people together with guidance on how to be an effective people manager. It should help them underpin their practice with sound, simply presented summaries of various theories and techniques.

The author has been a practising manager, primarily within the public sector, for a number of years and has worked her way up from junior management posts to director-level positions. Apart from her extensive leadership and managerial experience, she has studied the topic at both master's and doctorate levels. Her knowledge, skills and experience have been distilled into this book to provide aspiring and developing people managers with sound, basic understandings and guidance on the challenges of managing people within organizations.

What is people management?

Managers get things done through people, whether they are concerned with developing and selling services, or making and selling manufactured products. People managers work in all functions of a business and, apart from manufacturing products or providing services for customers, they can be involved with delivering services internally for other parts of the business. For example, the human resources and finance functions often provide services for other parts of the business or organization, and sometimes charge for these services. Finance, HR, communications, IT, sales, marketing and operational managers all use people to develop, make and sell services or products.

Managers in various functions have to manage people in order to deliver and meet work objectives. These people may work in the unit or team for which the people manager is responsible or be others within or outside the organization, such as contractors.

Effective people management is vital to the success of any business and the efficient functioning of organizations. There are many views on what makes a good people manager so we will be summarizing these and looking at what makes a poor people manager.

Today we will develop an understanding of:

The concept of people management

How people management relates to leadership

The debate around whether management is an art, science or profession

What makes a good people manager

The concept of people management

There are numerous views on what constitutes people management. It is difficult to define because there is no general agreement as to what people managers do. Fundamentally, people management is about organizing human and other resources to achieve efficient performance in meeting an organization's objectives. It is about making sure that employees are able to deliver the services or products of a company or organization within required timescales and to a satisfactorily high standard. It has been defined as the process of controlling and monitoring people through leading, motivating and inspiring individuals within teams, which may vary in size. In addition, people management is about ensuring that staff have the necessary knowledge, skills, experience, aptitudes and attitudes to perform in their allocated jobs. People managers also have a responsibility to look after the health and welfare of those they manage, and to provide developmental support.

It is accepted that people are the biggest asset of any enterprise and that success is very much dependent on the quality of employees. People management is not an easy task. Those in the role are expected to lead, motivate, inspire and encourage people who will in all probability have differing abilities, attitudes and behaviours. The people manager needs to know and understand individual members of his or her team in order to get the best out of them. He or she is also likely to be involved in recruiting, appraising, disciplining and dismissing staff.

The role of a people manager can vary considerably according to the size and the nature of the business. For example, those working in small businesses may need to be more adaptable and flexible in their roles due to the limited staff resources available, while those in larger organizations will have more clearly defined roles and may be expected to work in hierarchical structures and according to bureaucratic processes, as in public sector organizations. We will be covering the work of people managers in more detail on Monday.

Service-related business-to-customer businesses demand people managers who are highly skilled in client relationships and who have excellent negotiation and conflict resolution skills. Business-to-business manufacturing and service delivery companies require people managers who are able to understand the clients' business challenges, are good at negotiation and able to manage the relationships effectively. In creative and new media companies, normally there are less formal organizational structures so people managers need to know how to ensure that the culture and climate of the enterprise enables innovation and inspiration to flourish. This means creating the space and the right environment to allow creative ideas to emerge for commercial exploitation.

A well-known writer on organizations, Henry Mintzberg, identified ten distinct roles for managers and categorized these into decision-making, interpersonal and information processing. Each of these involves engaging with people in order to make the right decisions, maintaining effective working relationships and gaining the information necessary to carry out the job. However, people managers generally have more loosely defined jobs than those they manage and are in a position to make choices about the style and content of their jobs. They have more responsibility to make judgements, balance arguments and take decisions.

There is an ongoing debate about the differences between the leadership and management of people. A number of people claim that there are distinctive differences between management and leadership. They maintain that management has the following features.

- It is process-driven and about compliance.
- It involves controlling people, their work and time.
- It is about doing things properly and accomplishing things.
- It involves information-processing for decision-making.
- It is characterized by predictability and order.
- Communication is key, particularly informal communication through meetings, telephone calls and email.
- It is concerned with troubleshooting, solving ad hoc problems and resolving conflict.

● It is people-orientated and requires an understanding of the unique abilities and characteristics of those with whom a manager interacts in order to manage relationships for the good of the business.

Others believe that leadership is different from management because it involves:

● directing and guiding an organization or function
● scanning the external environment
● setting and articulating the organizational vision and strategy
● mobilizing employees through tapping into their emotions
● empowerment of the workforce
● influencing staff and stakeholders
● making sound judgements
● driving change and organizational transformation.

Regardless of the debate about whether someone is a leader or manager, there is evidence to show that people cannot be neatly categorized into the role of leader or manager. All management and leadership involve people, and most leaders manage and most managers lead. The extent to which people managers lead or manage is often dependent on how the individual concerned decides to carry out the role and the particular situation. Generally, less senior people managers are focused on operational issues, while those higher up in an organization tend to be more concerned with directing, influencing and guiding.

There has also been an ongoing debate about whether people management is an art, science or profession. However, what is clear is that management is about getting things done within businesses and organizations, even though it may apply science and use art to provide insights and vision. It cannot be properly defined as a profession because it cannot be learned formally in the same way as other professions such as the law, accountancy and engineering. Management involves people whose behaviours and actions cannot be predicted and situations which cannot be foreseen. People management is, therefore, a practice that is learned and developed through experience within particular contexts or environments. It is an intuitive process that involves taking action, reflecting and continual learning. The 'people manager' often subconsciously absorbs various signals and experiences to inform his or her decision-making and future practice.

The features of people management

People management takes place at all levels of an organization and in all functions, as organizations cannot deliver without people. Managers are found at first-line supervisory levels, where they are mainly concerned with ensuring that a small team is delivering its tasks to time and to a satisfactory quality. These roles are often relatively well-defined, but nevertheless provide plenty of scope for deciding how to manage individual team members and the team as a whole. There is also scope for first-line managers to contribute to the wider aims of companies and organizations as they are closest to the customer and in a position to obtain first-hand information about customer needs and how services can be improved. Junior managers are often protected from the politics of organizations and wider business stresses. They are frequently expected just to ensure that workers deliver services or products efficiently and effectively.

Generally, middle-line managers are those that are responsible for managing a few teams or, within a relatively small enterprise, a function. Their roles are more challenging as they are often expected to contribute to the wider objectives of the organization and are answerable to senior management and directors for the performance of their teams or the business function. They relate upwards to senior managers and directors and downwards to their teams within their operational or functional areas as well as maintaining relationships with managers in other related areas of the business and clients and customers.

Senior managers or directors tend to be regarded as the leaders of enterprises. They are the ones that create the vision and strategy for the organization and carry out top-level communication with key stakeholders, including those that may have a financial interest in the business. Middle managers usually report to them on the performance of functional and service areas. Senior and director post holders are expected to take the key decisions for a business's survival and growth.

The qualities of a people manager

Successful people managers possess a range of qualities, many of which are vital to the role. For example, a people manager who does not possess excellent interpersonal skills and have empathy with people is unlikely to be effective in motivating staff to give of their best in delivering business objectives. Furthermore, a people manager whose behaviour is inconsistent and displays moodiness will inevitably fail to achieve first-rate performance from staff. Good personality, social skills, understanding and emotional stability are therefore fundamental to the role of a people manager.

A people manager needs to be personable and accessible to staff at all times. He or she should take time to know the staff and be understanding and sympathetic to any personal issues that may impact on attendance and performance. However, clear boundaries need to be maintained between the people manager and team members, as people managers have the tough task of continually having to balance the needs of the work with those of individuals. There is no easy solution to this challenge as it is individual and situation dependent. However, the people manager needs to be fair, open and consistent in the way all staff are treated.

It is important not to try too hard to be popular by pleasing staff members. People managers should exercise tough love. While it is good to be liked, for a people manager it is more important to be respected. Respect does not come as a result of your position as a people manager, it has to be earned. Treating all staff with respect and fairness will help in establishing your reputation as a good people manager.

Continual communication is key to successful people management. Communication needs to be clear and concise, and delivered in an open and transparent way. People quickly pick up on insincerity and dishonesty, so any people manager who fails to be honest and sincere will quickly lose respect and it will be very difficult to regain this.

People need to be trusted to do their jobs and will react badly to being micro-managed. Successful people managers delegate effectively and stretch staff to perform to the best of their abilities and capabilities. They give regular praise for a job well done and constructive feedback when improvements are needed. They should also be open to receiving feedback on their own performance and acting on that feedback. People will respect you even more if you are prepared to acknowledge your own mistakes and put them right.

While a certain level of intelligence is important in any managerial role, this on its own does not make a good people manager. A people manager needs to know how to use intelligence and apply this with common sense. He or she needs to be knowledgeable about the business and the team's work, and continually imparting this knowledge to the team in an open and transparent way. The only situation where this should not happen is when the people manager may be aware of sensitive or confidential information that would be harmful to the business or its people if leaked out. The people manager should protect the team by also managing upwards and protecting his or her team from problems that more senior managers may be grappling with.

Poor people managers are uncommunicative, vague, lack good social skills, are distrustful of staff and delegate work ineffectively. They frequently change their minds. People respond negatively to such behaviours and will therefore not perform to their maximum competence. There are numerous features of successful and unsuccessful people management. Examples of such features are listed below.

Successful people managers	Unsuccessful people managers
Energize and motivate teams	Adopt a narrow interpretation of their role
Encourage excellence and initiate change	Focus on outputs at the expense of people
Inspire trust	Are excessively controlling
Resolve conflicts amicably	Avoid dealing with conflict
Align values and behaviours to corporate goals	Display unethical values
Adapt their management styles to situations	Adopt one management style for all situations

Delegate with support according to capacity and ability	Fail to delegate key tasks and micro-manage
Develop and coach people	Are reluctant to share their knowledge and skills
Seek feedback and act on it	Avoid asking for feedback
Communicate clearly and effectively	Are vague communicators
Develop responsive interpersonal relationships	Frequently 'divide and rule', thereby fostering internal competition among team members
Are visible and available	Are inaccessible and disengaged from the team
Lead by example	Display unacceptable behaviours
Openly praise staff and give credit for achievements	Rarely provide positive feedback and take personal credit for team's achievements
Are even-handed in their treatment of people	Treat people differently
Surround themselves with able people	Select mediocre staff who are unthreatening
Are accountable upwards and downwards	Are focused mainly on impressing senior management

SUNDAY
MONDAY
TUESDAY
WEDNESDAY
THURSDAY
FRIDAY
SATURDAY

Summary

Today has been about understanding the basic concept of people management, the role of the people manager and the importance of people management to the success or failure of organizations. We have discussed the differences between leadership and management. The debate around whether people management is an art, science or profession has also been explored and we have concluded that it is primarily a practice.

We have also looked at the differences in managerial responsibilities at various levels within organizations and undertaken a comparison of the features of successful and poor people managers.

You have now been provided with a fundamental understanding of what people management is about and a broad appreciation of how it relates to leadership. Tomorrow we will explore what people managers do in more depth.

SUNDAY
MONDAY
TUESDAY
WEDNESDAY
THURSDAY
FRIDAY
SATURDAY

Fact-check (answers at the back)

1. People management is about:
   a) Selling ❑
   b) Designing ❑
   c) Organizing and controlling ❑
   d) Public relations ❑

2. The success of a business is primarily dependent on:
   a) The product/services ❑
   b) Sales ❑
   c) Finance ❑
   d) People ❑

3. Mintzberg's ten roles of people managers are *not* categorized into:
   a) Directing ❑
   b) Decision-making ❑
   c) Information-processing ❑
   d) Interpersonal ❑

4. The people manager's job is:
   a) Loosely defined ❑
   b) Clearly defined ❑
   c) Undefined ❑
   d) Prescriptive ❑

5. A feature of management is:
   a) Environment scanning ❑
   b) Initiating change ❑
   c) Controlling people ❑
   d) Developing strategy ❑

6. A feature of leadership is:
   a) Information processing ❑
   b) Constant and organized ❑
   c) Directing and empowerment ❑
   d) Informal communication ❑

7. People management is:
   a) An art ❑
   b) A science ❑
   c) A profession ❑
   d) A practice ❑

8. People managers are found at:
   a) First-line supervisory level ❑
   b) Middle management level ❑
   c) Director level ❑
   d) All levels ❑

9. People managers at supervisory level:
   a) Develop strategy ❑
   b) Take key business decisions ❑
   c) Motivate teams ❑
   d) Manage several teams ❑

10. Successful people managers:
    a) Have high intellects ❑
    b) Manage detail ❑
    c) Are concerned about process ❑
    d) Have excellent social skills ❑

MONDAY

What do people managers do?

Today, we will explore in detail the role of people managers and the challenges they face. The key functions of team selection, directing and focusing staff, dealing with problems and issues, monitoring and controlling performance, developing the team and liaising with middle management will be covered.

As stated in the Sunday chapter, people management is not easy. There is no prescription or guide book that can teach you the practice adequately because all individuals are unique. They bring to the workplace their particular experiences and behaviours in the same way as you, their current or prospective manager. Furthermore, every management situation is different. You rarely get the same situation arising more than once so you continually have to apply your knowledge, skills, experience and intuition to each particular situation.

People managers recruit and manage staff often with the help of a human resources department. They also motivate and direct teams to deliver the organization's objectives efficiently and effectively. As part of their role they are expected to build and develop teams to perform to the best of their abilities and deal with problems, issues and conflicts.

Today, we are going to look in more detail at:

The various tasks of people managers

What people management actually involves

The role of a people manager

People managers are in positions of power. They have power, authority and influence over the daily working life of their team members. The use or abuse of this power can have either positive or negative impacts on people and therefore the business.

As a people manager, you have a responsibility to reflect on your behaviour to ensure that it is continually making staff feel that they are making a useful contribution and that you are always there for them in times of difficulty. You have the challenge of maintaining your team's enthusiasm and commitment, regardless of the pressures you or they may be under. This is not an easy task. While you can control yourself, many of the problems among the people you manage are outside your control. These problems can be many and varied. They frequently relate to people's lives outside the office. For example, the pressures of the arrival of a new baby, sickness in the family, money problems, relationship worries or health issues can all impact on a person's performance at work. These problems cannot be resolved by you, but you may be able to contain them using your power and influence to make it easier for the individuals concerned to deal with their problems.

There may also be relationship or motivational problems within the team that you will need to deal with on a day-to-day basis. Good communication, listening, mediation and influencing skills together with a fair and open approach to issues are vital in such situations. Staff will always respect a people manager who has taken the time to understand the issue, hear both sides and take tough and fair decisions. Effective use of your power and influence can have a positive impact on individuals and their particular problems, and improve the overall functioning of the team.

The role and functions of people managers can vary considerably depending on the sector they work in or their specialism. However, there are tasks which are common to nearly all people managers, such as:

- selecting the right team, where there is scope to do so
- directing and focusing the team on their individual and the team's goals and objectives

- monitoring and controlling performance
- dealing with any problems or issues that may arise
- managing conflict
- coaching and developing the team, while understanding an individual's particular learning style
- liaising with middle management.

We are going to cover how these activities should be approached, together with the challenges people managers are likely to face in carrying out these functions.

Selecting the right team

Sometimes, people managers have little choice over the recruitment of staff. They may inherit a team that has already been formed, be given employees from elsewhere in the organization, or offered members of staff who have been recruited by the HR department. Therefore, you may not have much scope to recruit and select your own team. You could inherit a fully staffed team that has been in existence for some time, a team that is subject to some change in which there are vacancies or a team that needs to be built from scratch. Regardless, you are likely to be involved in the recruitment and selection of staff at some point. When recruiting and selecting staff it is important to work closely with the organization's HR department or professionals in order to ensure the appropriate recruitment processes are followed and that you stick to the company's employment policies.

If you inherit a team that has been in existence for some time, it is probable that they will have well-established roles and ways of working. You will need to take time to understand the way people work and interact with each other before identifying and introducing any changes. If you decide to make changes it will be important to communicate to everyone the reasons and take account of their views before making any final decisions. In cases where you propose to go ahead with changes, you should justify why and reassure staff that any comments they have made have been fully taken into account.

In the case of vacancies within a team, you may recruit for these either through internal or external advertising. Whichever method of advertising you use, you will need to draw up a job and person specification in consultation with the HR function. The former will need to cover the tasks required, while the latter will set out the particular knowledge, skills, experience and behaviours needed for the post. Examples are presented below.

Job description

Job title: Marketing Manager

Location: Sales and Marketing Team, Headquarters, Oldtown

Reporting arrangements: Position reports to the Sales and Marketing Manager.

Job purpose: To implement the marketing plan and manage the marketing budget.

Key responsibilities and accountabilities:

Management of two marketing executives and one administrator.

Management of financial budget.

Draw up and implement a marketing plan for the business.

Advise senior management on marketing and PR in relation to key strategic objectives.

Organize marketing campaigns.

Approve press notices and media features.

Develop, implement and monitor an internal communications strategy.

Undertake market research.

Draft tenders, select and manage advertising and PR agencies.

Prepare and implement a social marketing strategy.

Monitor and evaluate marketing activities.

Dated:

Person specification	
Qualities, skills and experience	**How criteria will be assessed**
Minimum of two years' managerial function within a marketing department (E)	Application and interview
Strong, effective communicator (E)	Presentation and interview
Good team-working skills (E)	Interview
Ability to see the big picture and contribute to marketing of company top-level strategic aims (E)	Interview
Excellent written skills (E)	Application and written test
Experience of external public relations activities (D)	Application, written test and interview
Experience of internal communications (D)	Application, written test and interview
Knowledge of monitoring and evaluation techniques (E)	Interview
Experience in social marketing and website development (E)	Application and interview
Competent in market research methodologies (E)	Interview
Management experience of marketing campaigns (E)	Application and interview
Experience of managing external PR and advertising agencies (D)	Application and interview
Personal characteristics and attitude	Application, interview and references
Pleasant, sociable and enthusiastic	
Displays commitment, flexibility and adaptability	
Clean driving licence and willing to be away from home overnight	
Educational requirements	Application and certificates
Degree in relevant discipline (E)	
Masters degree in marketing or business (D)	

(E) essential; (D) desirable

The selection process provides an opportunity for you to explore and identify whether the applicant has the necessary requisites for the job and to assess their suitability for the particular position. The aim is to find the best matched person for the post. Applications should be measured objectively against the requirements set out in the job and person specifications in order to select candidates for testing (if needed) and interviewing. Following sifting of applications, interviews should be held to assess applicants' suitability for the job and how well they would fit into the team and culture of the organization. The same process would be followed for establishing an entirely new team. However, in such cases you should consider carefully the mix of skills, personal qualities and characteristics necessary to establish a well-functioning team, in particular the diversity of team members. It is customary to seek written references for candidates but these can be unreliable for a number of reasons so it is often worthwhile speaking informally to previous employers and character referees to gain a more accurate picture of the individual's performance and behaviour in the workplace and socially.

Job descriptions and accompanying person specifications are useful documents for people managers. They can serve many purposes, such as:

- giving job applicants a clear description of the role
- setting out what is expected of team members
- providing a basis for measuring performance
- providing a useful document for settling any disputes between the people manager and a particular team member
- identifying areas for training and development
- providing an essential reference document for dealing with disciplinary issues
- providing an objective basis for performance reviews and appraisals.

All new recruits should be given an induction which covers basics rules and guidance on subjects such as:

- working times, holiday and sick leave allowances
- coffee breaks and lunch arrangements
- the dress code

- location of the toilets
- the organization's vision, mission, goals and values
- HR policies, health and safety, diversity and environmental policies and practices
- the job expectations.

An induction training plan should be given to the new staff member either before or immediately they start work. Taking new entrants into the business through an induction programme will help settle them in quickly so they become productive in a relatively short time as well as contributing to their retention and reducing dependence on you as a people manager. As part of the induction process, new staff members should also have a full briefing on the job they are expected to do, the processes to be followed and timescales for delivery of overall expectations. We touch upon this point in more depth in the following section on directing and focusing the team.

Directing and focusing the team

Each individual within the team should have a job description, which sets out the tasks required of them. They should be clear about what is expected of them and how their roles relate to individual, team and organizational goals and performance targets. These targets can be many and varied, according to the particular function of the team and/or individual. They could relate to the number of products manufactured or processed, the number of products or services sold, the number of marketing opportunities exploited, the number of internal customers helped with problems and so on. Targets should relate to the overall business plan/strategy for the organization or functional area. At an individual level, targets should be included in annual performance management plans (see the Friday chapter).

As a people manager, it is your job to make sure that all teams members meet or exceed their targets in terms of numbers, required quality and timescales. It is, therefore, vital that all your team members have a clear understanding of the expectations of them and the team as a whole. Poor communication is the cause of many of the problems that arise in teams. Staff need to be fully aware of:

● the scope of their responsibilities and how they are accountable for them

- the organizational values and culture
- the level of knowledge and skills expected for the role
- the actions to be undertaken
- the expected attitudes and behaviours
- the performance levels expected in terms of both quality and quantity.

Apart from ensuring that staff are aware of the above points, people managers need to deploy a range of skills to encourage, influence and motivate team members to deliver what is required of them. Later in the week, we will look in more detail at some aspects of the skills and behaviours of successful people managers such as appropriate management styles and motivational theories.

Neither people nor work situations are stable and predictable. Consequently, the people manager's role is ever-and fast-changing, and challenging. It is vital, therefore, that you, as a manager of people, reflect continually on the dynamics of various situations, in particular your own reactions and behaviours, and take action in response to this reflective practice. This is necessary for maintaining the harmony and output of the team, in addition to continuing with your own personal development in order to refine your qualities and skills to become an excellent and even more successful people manager.

Dealing with problems and issues

Day-to-day problems and issues will arise continually. It will often be your responsibility to resolve these. The nature and sources of these can vary considerably. Involving your team in sorting out problems is a smart move as they will feel you value their capabilities and opinions. This is the case in relation to both those problems you can solve and those that you may find difficult. You can do this by:

- seeking views on the problem or issue
- exploring with staff the options for dealing with the problem
- asking for recommendations.

Another advantage for you, as a people manager, in involving your staff in resolving problems and addressing issues is that they are also more likely to come to you with suggestions for improving the business, which will help build your credibility with senior management. Furthermore, staff retention is likely to remain at a relatively high level if people are feeling appreciated for their contributions to problem-solving.

Managing conflict

As a people manager, it is inevitable that you will have to deal with conflict as part of your day-to-day work. Conflict may arise between you and team members or between you and senior management. There may also be conflict between team members that you will need to resolve. On average you could find yourself spending about a day a week or more on managing conflict and trying to find resolutions. Conflict affects team morale, productivity, profit and customer relationships. If unresolved it can lead to legal proceedings, which are costly in terms of time, money and the organization's reputation. It is therefore worthwhile for the people manager to learn about the many causes of conflict and the best way to manage it.

For example, conflict can arise if:

- someone feels they are being treated unfairly
- they are asked to do something that does not suit them for one reason or another
- there is a clash of values and/or beliefs
- there is competition for limited resources.

The source of conflict may not necessarily relate to the work of the organization, as personal issues can also sometimes lead to conflict in the workplace.

Conflict can either be healthy or unhealthy for a business. Healthy conflict is when there is disagreement about a decision or course of action which necessitates the parties involved having to set out the arguments and explore each perspective in order to reach a reasoned decision or agreement. The process is useful for discussing all options, the risks involved and the benefits and drawbacks. The parties agree without acrimony and action is taken to move matters forward. Unhealthy conflict, however, can be very damaging for businesses. It needs to be managed and resolved quickly in order to minimize adverse impacts.

Conflict resolution is about dealing with the source of the conflict and agreeing action to eliminate or reduce it. As a people manager, you can deal with conflict through negotiation, dominance, compromise, influence, bargaining, mediation, arbitration or avoidance. If the last strategy is employed, unless one or other party leaves the business, the likelihood is that the conflict situation will worsen and be even more damaging for the organization. Furthermore, it is unlikely that dominance would lead to a resolution that would make people feel valued and good about themselves. Negotiation, compromise and influence are the most effective strategies. If these are unsuccessful, you would need to resort to mediation or arbitration.

The first stage, if possible, is to identify whether there are any signs of conflict within the team or between individual team members. The indications may be a noticeable falling off of support for new work, poor response to discussions and limited input into meetings. Other signs include a fall in productivity, higher than normal sickness leave and negative behaviours. If you suspect that there is a problem the important thing is to address it before the conflict escalates. If not addressed early, the likelihood is that there will be some obvious signs of conflict such as unresolved arguments, lack of cooperation or goodwill, or refusals to support other team members. Once you realize that conflict is present within the team and you are aware of the parties concerned, which could involve you, the next stage is to identify its root cause.

The causes of conflict are many and varied. They include:

● weak management
● unfair or unequal treatment
● lack of clarity in job roles
● inadequate guidance or training

- poor working conditions
- bullying behaviour and harassment by management or a team member
- unrealistic expectations.

This may not necessarily be easy, but it is important that you acknowledge the symptoms as quickly as possible and take further action.

Once the cause of conflict has been identified, you will need to find a resolution that is satisfactory to all parties involved. Your organization may well have an established policy or procedure for handling conflict, which you should follow in such circumstances. Often the issue can be sorted out quickly and amicably on an informal basis without having to resort to formal procedures. If unsuccessful at the informal stage, you will need to follow formal processes in close consultation with your HR department in order to avoid an employment tribunal claim or industrial action.

When conflict is first recognized it may be sufficient to simply monitor the situation as the parties concerned often resolve the matter themselves or move on. However, if a minor disagreement or personality clash persists or escalates you will need to intervene by having a quiet word with both sides, making each aware of the situation and how they can achieve their own goals without clashing with others. Use of your negotiation and influencing skills will be key and you may possibly need to find a compromise solution. If, as the people manager, you fail to sort out the conflict, you could consider asking for the advice or intervention of your senior manager. In cases where conflict problems appear to be developing into a major issue, it is beneficial to consider bringing in an independent mediator before going through formal processes which could be costly and damaging for the business.

Monitoring and controlling performance

As a people manager, you will carry responsibility for setting the team's and individual members' targets. Targets need to relate to wider business objectives and cover both quantity and quality of work produced. Deciding performance targets is not an easy task as they can have a considerable effect on team and individual motivation. If targets are too demanding and almost impossible to achieve, this will be demoralizing for staff. They will feel that no matter how hard they work, they will never be able to achieve what is expected of them. If targets are set too low, individuals and the team will not be stretched, and their sense of achievement will be diminished. It is, therefore, important for staff satisfaction and business success that you determine targets that stretch the team and are demanding, while ensuring that staff will be motivated to achieve them. Targets need to be achievable and measurable, in line with the SMART concept:

S – Specific
M – Measurable
A – Attainable
R – Relevant
T – Time-bound

Involving your team in setting and agreeing targets is a worthwhile exercise as they will feel that they are having some influence over the process and have ownership of the targets. You may need to negotiate these targets with higher management. If so, involvement of the team in this process should help you with providing senior management with the case and evidence for setting targets at particular levels.

Targets can be set daily, weekly, monthly or annually. There are often numerous internal or external factors that may impact on their achievement. For example, targets can be impacted through a new contract won or a contract lost, a supplier going out of business, supply problems, the absence of critical staff or a change in business direction due to external factors. Targets, therefore, need to be kept under review and, if necessary and appropriate, revised at regular intervals.

In order to control the achievement of targets, continual monitoring has to take place at regular, appropriate intervals. The timescales for monitoring targets will vary according to the nature of the work and the business. Monitoring can be done by a variety of methods, such as email communication, use of spreadsheets, reporting formats or through meetings. If progress is satisfactory and there is no need for any enquiry into failure to meet targets, the process can probably be effectively executed through email or paper communication. However, if there is significant over- or under-achievement of targets it may be necessary to hold a meeting with staff and possibly other representatives of the business to review the reasons, agree actions and amend the targets as necessary. Regular communication with the team is important in respect of any of the above monitoring methods. People need to know how well they are doing and whether they need to improve in any areas in order to meet or exceed targets.

At an individual level, people are usually given targets as part of their annual performance plan, which should be reviewed by their managers at least twice a year. These targets link with work objectives and personal objectives that relate to how the person concerned should increase their knowledge, skills level and experience to perform in the job at a higher level. We will cover this process in more detail on Friday when we will talk about how to manage performance.

Developing the team

A people manager will inherit staff members from a variety of backgrounds, each of whom will have their own unique life experiences, behaviours, intelligence levels and aptitudes. Individuals will inevitably have varying levels of skills, knowledge and work experience as well as differing learning styles. We will be dealing with the topic of coaching and developing the team in more detail on Saturday. At this point, we will simply note the importance of a people manager developing coaching and mentoring skills in order to develop staff and improve their overall performance.

Liaising with middle management

No people manager operates in isolation of managers elsewhere in the business. There is usually someone to whom the people manager is accountable. This could be a middle level line manager or a senior manager or director. Usually, the performance targets for the team together with budget allocations are agreed with the supervising manager or director to whom the people manager reports regularly. A close working relationship should be developed with this individual in order for the team manager to appreciate and understand the pressures on the business. The opportunity should also be taken to suggest ways in which changes could be introduced to help overall business performance. These communications may be formal, such as regular meetings and reporting, or informal email communications, telephone conversations and face-to-face discussions. Keeping each other up to date and aware of any issues is vital to business survival and development.

As well as managing downwards, the people manager also needs to consider the need to manage upwards. Sometimes, senior managers can place unrealistic or unworkable demands on the people manager's teams and may interfere in the management process. In such situations, the people manager has an obligation to communicate effectively with senior management about what can be achieved or what is workable, providing evidence wherever possible, as part of a realistic case. It is important to look for solutions and answers to help the senior manager concerned achieve a satisfactory response to the issue before him or her. If there is a case of senior management interference in your management you should take steps to reaffirm your role and responsibilities diplomatically.

Summary

We have covered the power, authority and influence of people managers, and what they actually do in practice.

We have emphasized the importance of people managers exercising their power and influence effectively to help those in their teams deal with personal or work-related issues, as well as the importance of being open to listening and being prepared to take tough but fair decisions. The importance and cost effectiveness of a well-planned and delivered induction training programme for new recruits has also been covered.

The role of a people manager has been categorized into that of recruiter, director, problem-solver, conflict manager, target-setter, controller, performance manager, team developer and acting as the link between the team and more senior management.

Tomorrow we will look at the subject of motivation, which is a key challenge for people managers.

SUNDAY

MONDAY

TUESDAY

WEDNESDAY

THURSDAY

FRIDAY

SATURDAY

Fact-check (answers at the back)

1. Job and person specifications are written by:
   a) The HR department ❏
   b) The job-holder ❏
   c) The people manager ❏
   d) The team ❏

2. Targets will be defined in a:
   a) Job description ❏
   b) Person specification ❏
   c) Performance plan ❏
   d) Job advertisement ❏

3. In dealing with problems the people manager should:
   a) Seek help from staff ❏
   b) Refer to his or her manager ❏
   c) Resolve the issue ❏
   d) Leave it to others ❏

4. Targets need to be...? Complete the words.
   a) S...... ❏
   b) M...... ❏
   c) A...... ❏
   d) R...... ❏
   e) T...... ❏

5. Targets should be agreed with:
   a) The people manager ❏
   b) The team ❏
   c) Senior management ❏
   d) The organization ❏

6. Targets should be:
   a) Reviewed monthly ❏
   b) Reviewed weekly ❏
   c) Reviewed annually ❏
   d) Reviewed according to their nature and level ❏

7. Causes of conflict include:
   a) Strong management ❏
   b) Equality ❏
   c) Favouritism ❏
   d) Social events ❏

8. Effective ways of dealing with conflict are:
   a) Unilateral decisions ❏
   b) Dominant style ❏
   c) Leaving the parties to sort things out ❏
   d) Listening and negotiating ❏

9. Individual performance targets should be:
   a) Reviewed weekly ❏
   b) Reviewed monthly ❏
   c) Reviewed annually ❏
   d) Reviewed every six months ❏

10. A people manager is:
   a) Only responsible for the team ❏
   b) Responsible for managing his/her manager ❏
   c) Responsible for managing upwards and downwards ❏
   d) Responsible for managing across the organization ❏

TUESDAY

Motivating people in the workplace

The topic of motivation of staff is of prime interest to people managers. A number of well-known theories on the motivation of people have been developed in the past half-century or so, and they remain relevant in today's work situations. Today we are going to learn about the work of the prominent writers on the subject and touch upon more recent motivational work, which tends to be based on the original theories.

First, we will cover the work of Abraham Maslow, who developed a hierarchy of motivational needs. His work was developed further by Frederick Herzberg's motivation hygiene theory and David McClelland's motivational needs theory, which will also be discussed. The work of Douglas McGregor will be touched upon because it is relatively controversial. He has maintained that in respect of motivation, people are divided into those who are not interested in work and those who are keen to work. He classifies these as types X and Y respectively, which gave rise to the theory's name.

Today you will learn about:

The key motivational theories in relation to people in the workplace

The importance of understanding these theories in order to manage people effectively

How people's motivational drivers can differ according to a number of factors

How you can use motivational knowledge to tap into the individual's motivational needs in order to get them to achieve work objectives

The importance of understanding motivational theories

Motivation within the workplace can be explained as the extent to which individuals want to engage in certain behaviours and actions that meet their personal needs in relation to work. All people have different needs and goals. They behave and act in a way that leads to meeting these needs and goals. The most successful organizations tend to have highly motivated workers. This is shown in terms of high productivity, high quality work with little wastage, quick responses to issues and employees being encouraged, and even required, to give feedback and make improvement suggestions.

Motivating the people you manage is a challenging task but fundamental to your effectiveness as a people manager. In order to motivate people, you need to have an understanding of the basic motivational theories, the personal motivations of various individuals for whom you have management responsibility, and techniques for applying the theories in order to help staff maximize their performance.

There are several well-known motivational theories. Although these were developed decades ago, they remain very relevant in today's workplace. Maslow's hierarchy of needs is one that is frequently referred to, as is Herzberg's motivation hygiene theory and McClelland's motivational needs theory. Another renowned theory, about which there is some debate, is Douglas McGregor's X and Y theory.

There is a view that people managers perform best when they focus on employee engagement to understand them as individuals, their particular motivations and recognize their achievements. Therefore, people managers need a basic understanding of motivational theories and to learn how to apply them in the right circumstances in order to maintain and increase the motivation of their staff.

Maslow's hierarchy of needs

Abraham Maslow developed his hierarchy of needs model during the 1940s and 1950s. It is based on the idea that it is the responsibility of employers to provide a workplace environment that encourages and enables staff members to fulfil their potential, which is referred to as self-actualization. He developed a hierarchy of needs based on five motivational stages, which are frequently presented as a pyramid diagram.

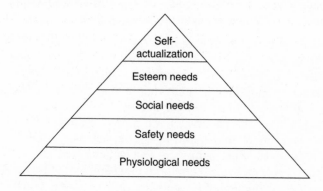

Maslow recognized that we are all motivated by needs, the most basic of which deals with our survival needs and is termed in the model as physiological (or biological) needs. He maintained that people's needs have to be satisfied according to the order given in the model. Maslow was of the view that only when the lower order needs are satisfied do we move on to the higher order needs.

In order to meet our physiological needs we seek the basic living requirements of food, water, air, shelter and sleep. Once this first need has been satisfied, people move on to satisfy their higher safety needs of keeping themselves and their families protected, secure and stable. The next stage in the hierarchy is social needs, which relate to belongingness and love within the family, other relationships and from the workplace. Once these needs are met we move on to meet our esteem needs, which are about our achievements, status, responsibilities and reputations. Finally, we seek self-actualization through personal growth and fulfilment.

The criticisms of Maslow's theory are that:

- individuals' behaviours respond to more than one need
- people may employ different behaviours in response to the same need
- it is not easy to decide when a need has been satisfied
- people's behaviours are far more complex than this model allows for and are affected by life experiences and events, and their frame of mind in certain situations.

A failure of someone to have their needs satisfied usually leads to stress and a decline in their work performance. As a people manager you need to have an understanding of this model together with knowledge about your staff in order to appreciate why someone is not performing as well as they could and failing to fulfil their potential. For example, if a team member is earning enough to meet his or her physiological needs but is in debt and his or her home is at risk (safety needs), it will not be possible to motivate them through feeling part of the work team (belongingness and love needs) and giving them further responsibilities (esteem needs). As a manager you will need to find ways within your power to help that individual meet his or her safety needs. This could be done through the offer of overtime, an interest-free company loan or debt counselling.

Herzberg's motivation hygiene theory

Frederick Herzberg's motivation hygiene theory claims that the factors which motivate people at work are different from and not simply polar opposites of the factors which cause dissatisfaction. Job satisfiers are about the factors involved in doing the job, while the job 'dis-satisfiers' are the factors which define the job context. There are similarities between Herzberg's and Maslow's theories as Herzberg argued that people's hygiene needs need to be satisfied before they can be motivated to perform well in the workplace. Examples of Herzberg's hygiene needs and how they relate to Maslow's hierarchy of needs are:

Herzberg's hygiene factors	Maslow's hierarchy of needs
Organizational policy	Safety needs
Work conditions	Safety needs
Relationship with manager	Belongingness and love needs
Salary	Physiological and safety needs
Benefits	Safety needs
Status	Esteem needs
Security	Safety needs
Relationships with colleagues	Belongingness and love needs
Personal life	Physiological, safety, belongingness and love needs

Herzberg's view was that the satisfaction of the hygiene factors was a prerequisite to motivating people through what he termed the true motivators:

● achievement
● recognition
● the work itself
● responsibility
● advancement.

Although similar to Maslow's model, Herzberg maintained that only the higher level needs of Maslow's hierarchy act as motivators, while the lower order needs are what he has termed as satisfiers, i.e. the hygiene factors. Management must, therefore, meet the hygiene factors in order to avoid employee dissatisfaction and the effects of this on the business. To motivate staff, Herzberg considered that job enhancement or enrichment factors should be introduced to tap into the intrinsic motivational drivers within individuals.

As a people manager you have some, but not complete, control or influence over the satisfiers. You are able to develop relationships with staff and foster good relationships between team members and others in the organization. You may also be able to influence salary and benefits, and possibly contribute to improvements in working conditions and organizational policies in a way that will help satisfy the needs of staff.

However, you will have little or no influence on the hygiene factors of job security and people's personal lives.

However, generally a people manager is able to use Herzberg's true motivators. For example, we discussed in Monday's chapter the importance of setting targets which relate to a person's achievements. These targets should be demanding, but not too hard so that individuals will feel that they have failed if they are not met. If targets are too easy, individuals will not feel stretched, which through lack of achievement could lead to feelings of unworthiness or not feeling valued. People need to be praised for their achievements and contributions at regular intervals and exceptional successes should be celebrated. This should be a regular feature of the people manager's role.

Another example is recognition, which is about being appreciated for your contribution to the team and the business. This may frequently relate to achievement of work objectives or contributions to the team or organization, which can come in many forms, such as:

- coming up with innovative ideas to improve organizational functioning
- supporting a colleague who may be struggling in carrying out a task
- arranging a social event
- volunteering to represent the business in your spare time
- going that extra mile for an internal or external customer.

It is important to show members of your team that you care and appreciate it when they do something well or outside their normal duties. It is also worthwhile letting others in the organization know about how well individuals are performing and when they are delivering over and above expectations.

As regards the work itself, people generally want interesting and challenging work in order to feel engaged and interested and to have a sense of achievement. Depending on the nature of your business, you may have limited scope to create interesting work. However, there are ways in which you can redesign jobs to make them less routine and you can share out the more mundane tasks among team members, including yourself. If staff see that you are also bearing a share of the routine work, their respect for you will increase and they will be more inclined to support you in times of crisis.

Responsibility is a positive motivator because if you assign responsibility to someone it implies you value and trust them. However, you need to be confident that the person to whom you are assigning responsibility has the competence, confidence and capacity to carry out the additional responsibilities. You also need to be sure that the action will not make other members of the team feel disgruntled.

Advancement usually refers to promotion, salary increase and improved job prospects. In order to achieve advancement people need to show they have the capability to take on increased responsibilities, have acquired new skills, have developed their competencies and can make a contribution to the business at a higher level. The people manager has a responsibility to provide individual team members with job experience, skills development and learning opportunities that will help them advance their careers. We will be discussing people development on Saturday, but it should be noted that not everyone is interested in or has the capability for career advancement so the people manager needs to be sensitive to the motivational needs of these individuals and find other ways to motivate them in the job.

McClelland's motivational needs theory

David McClelland's motivational needs theory is closely related to the theories of Herzberg. McClelland was of the opinion that there are the following three types of motivational needs:

- achievement
- authority/power
- affiliation.

He maintained that all employees of organizations have these needs to varying degrees. He further argued that the extent to which they are inherent in an individual determines a person's or manager's style and behaviour in respect of their personal motivation and how they motivate others.

For example, the achievement-dominated individual is driven towards the accomplishment of challenging goals and career advancement. They need to carry out difficult but attainable tasks at a high level. These individuals need success and to be praised and recognized for their efforts and outcomes. Financial rewards, security and status are not prime motivators. Achievement-motivated people seek personal responsibility and can make good leaders, although they can be too results-driven and demand a lot from staff.

Those that seek power and authority are driven to be influential and to be viewed as leaders who have an impact, and tend to dominate with their ideas. They have a need to control others and like to be in charge so that they can direct and influence others to achieve organizational goals. Power- and authority-driven people enjoy status and competition. They tend to be demanding of others, articulate and ambitious for leadership positions. However, their quest for prestige can impact adversely on their actual performance in their jobs.

The affiliation-motivated person has a need for people interaction and to develop friendly relationships. They want to be liked and popular. These individuals make good team players as they want to be accepted and are inclined to conform to group norms. Affiliation-motivated people have a preference for cooperation over competition, and are good in customer service roles and jobs that involve client interaction. As a people manager you need to be aware that because of the dominant need to be popular, these types can undermine objectivity and your decision-making capability.

McClelland claimed that most people have and demonstrate a combination of the above characteristics, but a number exhibit a strong bias to one particular motivational need, which inevitably affects their workplace behaviours and management styles. There is a fair level of support for McClelland's theory. The challenge for people managers is in determining the levels of individual needs and subsequently matching these to a job situation.

McGregor's X and Y theory

Douglas McGregor proposed that there are just two fundamental approaches to people management and that people and their managers can, therefore, be categorized into two types.

- Those with a leaning toward type X, which is based on the assumption that on average people dislike and will avoid work if they can; they prefer to be directed; avoid responsibility; are relatively unambitious; and want security first and foremost. McGregor claimed that these people call for an authoritarian management style whereby the manager dictates what is required and uses the threat of punishment in order to get them to work towards organizational objectives. This particular management style rarely gets good results from people and can be the cause of discontent and absenteeism.
- Type Y people, are said to find that effort in work is natural and easy. They are self-controlled and self-directed in pursuit of organizational objectives. They seek and accept responsibility. They do not need to be controlled or to have the threat of punishment hanging over them. Type Y people have the capacity to apply innovation, creativity and imagination in solving an organization's problems. As managers they are participative and bring out the best in people.

We will be exploring management styles on Wednesday and this will include the features of both autocratic and participative managers.

It is claimed that type X workers are best motivated through rewards, while type Y people are believed to be motivated by being allowed to create environments in which staff can develop and flourish. Critics of McGregor's theory take the view that it is outdated in the light of the trend for self-managed teams and that it represents two behaviour extremes.

The challenge of motivating people

One of your principal tasks as a manager is to motivate your people. Knowledge of the theories above will help you identify the individual needs and characteristics of your staff and adopt the most appropriate motivator in order to get the best out of them at work. Depending on the individual and situation, you will need to apply a variety of people management styles, which we will cover on Wednesday. One particular style is unlikely to be effective in motivating a team of people, each with different personal characteristics and motivational drivers. There are numerous techniques you can apply, such as giving praise and constructive criticism, helping to build an individual's skills, giving more responsibility, providing learning and development opportunities, redesigning jobs to make them more interesting and monetary rewards, if this is within your power.

The people manager needs to be aware of the benefits and drawbacks of the dominant motivational characteristics in the staff he or she manages in order to place people in the roles that best suit them and best meet their motivational needs. As a people manager you need to be continually assessing the motivational needs of team members and managing them in a way that meets these needs so that they perform to the best of their abilities and are content in their jobs. It is also important for you to be aware of your particular motivational needs and to reflect on and adapt your behaviours and actions accordingly.

It is vitally important to:

- communicate clearly and regularly with your staff
- ask their views on how to improve the working situation
- arrange social events occasionally
- know your staff in order to gain insights into their personal lives
- be flexible with small gestures
- say thank you so people feel appreciated and not overlooked.

Summary

In order to build an appreciation and understanding of people's motivational needs, we have studied the main, well-known motivational theories of Maslow, Herzberg, McClelland and McGregor.

You have been given an example of how Maslow's hierarchy of needs theory could be applied in today's organizational settings, and shown how Herzberg's motivation hygiene theory is similar to Maslow's theory, along with McClelland's motivational needs theory. McGregor's X and Y theory takes a different approach by categorizing people into those who do not want to work (type X) and those who do and are keen to achieve (type Y). McGregor's theory is linked to differing management styles, which we are going to explore tomorrow.

SUNDAY
MONDAY
TUESDAY
WEDNESDAY
THURSDAY
FRIDAY
SATURDAY

Fact-check (answers at the back)

1. Physiological needs relate to:
a) Job security ☐
b) Team work ☐
c) Status ☐
d) Survival ☐

2. Self-actualization needs relate to:
a) Praise ☐
b) Social acceptance ☐
c) Personal growth ☐
d) Status ☐

3. X and Y theory was developed by:
a) Herzberg ☐
b) Maslow ☐
c) McGregor ☐
d) McClelland ☐

4. Hygiene factors include:
a) Security ☐
b) Responsibility ☐
c) Achievement ☐
d) Work content ☐

5. Herzberg's true motivators include:
a) Advancement ☐
b) Salary ☐
c) Status ☐
d) Work relationships ☐

6. Which of the following is *not* included in McClelland's theory?
a) Affiliation ☐
b) Authority/power ☐
c) Recognition ☐
d) Achievement ☐

7. Type X people:
a) Seek work ☐
b) Are ambitious ☐
c) Avoid responsibility ☐
d) Are self-motivated ☐

8. Theory Y people:
a) Like to be directed ☐
b) Seek security ☐
c) Need to be controlled ☐
d) Innovate ☐

9. McClelland's theory is:
a) Motivation hygiene ☐
b) Motivational needs ☐
c) Hierarchy of needs ☐
d) X and Y theory ☐

10. Herzberg's hygiene factor of relationships with colleagues links with Maslow's:
a) Safety needs ☐
b) Physiological needs ☐
c) Esteem needs ☐
d) Belongingness and love needs ☐

WEDNESDAY

People management styles

In the Tuesday chapter, we referred to the choice of people management styles when considering how to motivate staff. A management style reflects a people manager's preferred way of making decisions and controlling and relating to the work group.

People tend to have a dominant management style, although they can adopt differing styles for different situations. There are a number of accepted management styles, such as autocratic, democratic, paternalistic, bureaucratic etc. We are going to discuss the features of each of the most well-known styles today, together with their advantages and disadvantages. We will also be linking the motivational theories discussed on Tuesday to certain management styles and outlining situations in which particular styles would be appropriate.

At the end of today you should have an appreciation of:

different management styles

the pros and cons of using them in certain situations

People management styles

As shown on Monday, the work of people managers is multi-faceted. They have many roles to play in organizations and have to rely on people in order to complete tasks and deliver business objectives. How people managers carry out their roles and handle various situations depends on their management style, which can be constructive and positive, destructive and negative, or neutral and ineffectual in particular settings.

Today we are going to explore various management styles and their appropriateness for certain situations. As mentioned on Tuesday there are close links between people managers' particular management styles and their responsibilities for motivating staff.

Management styles relate to the characteristic ways in which people managers make decisions and relate to their staff. People tend to adopt a certain style according to their personal characteristics, life experiences and motivations. However, management style should be dependent on the particular circumstances of a situation. Good people managers will deploy a range of styles according to the people and work situations they are dealing with.

The most widely accepted forms of management styles are classed as:

- autocratic
- democratic
- bureaucratic
- consultative
- persuasive
- laissez-faire
- MBWA (management by walking about)
- paternalistic.

We are going to discuss the features of each of these and their advantages and disadvantages. We are also going to learn about the situations in which it may be appropriate to use them.

Autocratic

A people manager who is autocratic is inclined to take decisions without consulting those who may be affected or those who may hold an interest in the particular issue. Autocratic managers tend to make decisions and then expect staff to do exactly as they have been told. Little consideration is given to the impact of their decisions on others. There are two types of autocratic managers.

- A directive autocrat, who takes decisions unilaterally and expects staff to carry them out without argument and under close supervision.
- A permissive autocrat, who makes unilateral decisions but gives staff the freedom to decide how to carry out his or her instructions.

The decisions of either type will inevitably reflect the views and personality of the people manager concerned. On the positive side, an autocratic manager can be viewed as being confident and competent in managing the business. On the other hand, if those managed are strong and competent and fall into McGregor's Y category of people, they may well resent this approach and be resistant to accepting the decisions. This could lead to conflict within the group. Furthermore, this style tends to foster dependence on the manager.

There are occasions when this type of people management style may be appropriate, such as in times of crisis or when staff are inexperienced and do not have the capacity to contribute effectively to the decision-making process.

Democratic

The democratic people manager is at the opposite end of the spectrum to an autocratic manager. Democratic management is about full employee involvement and feedback. This type of manager involves everyone in the decision-making process and decisions are made on the basis of majority agreement. It involves extensive communication with those concerned. There are two types of democratic people managers: permissive and directive.

The former allows staff to carry out the decisions as they see fit, while the latter will be very involved with staff in carrying out decisions.

The advantages of a democratic style of manager are that staff will feel involved and valued, and the decisions made are likely to be acceptable to most of the team or work group. A democratic people management style can improve job satisfaction and the quality of work as well as generating enthusiastic ideas from staff. The disadvantages are that a considerable amount of time and effort is spent on decision-making which could possibly be used more profitably elsewhere in the business, and that there is no guarantee that the decisions will be in the best interest of the business. This particular form of management style is often useful in complex, major decision-making processes.

Bureaucratic

Bureaucratic management is found primarily in public sector bodies and many large corporate businesses, particularly those that are regulated. There is a need in these organizations for accountability and transparency to gain public confidence, the support of stakeholders and shareholders and the confidence of industry regulators. In such organizations the risks of contravening the law, regulations, policies and procedures are relatively high and could lead to critical or disastrous consequences, in particular for large private-sector enterprises or health and social care bodies. To protect the public or other stakeholders, it is necessary for such organizations to have in place efficient and effective recording processes and procedures to minimize mistakes, ensure adherence to any governing laws or regulations and achieve quality outputs. Such systems may mitigate any wrongdoing and have the foregoing benefits, although they are not foolproof. Other advantages include more reliable decision-making and safeguarding from abuse by employees or managers. Disadvantages of bureaucratic systems include slow decision-making and delivery, and they tend to be resource intensive and, therefore, costly.

Consultative

Although this type of management style implies worker involvement in decision-making, in effect it is dictatorial and similar to the autocratic style. The communication is usually from senior management to lower levels within the management chain for the purpose of seeking views and feedback on proposals. However, frequently the decisions have more or less been made, so the purpose of consulting is primarily to obtain the commitment of employees and maintain staff morale. The prime advantage of this style is that it can engender loyalty, although you should not underestimate the ability of employees to view the consultation as a pointless exercise. The disadvantages of this style are similar to those of the autocratic management style.

Persuasive

The persuasive management style is another that has similarities with the autocratic style, but with more emphasis on employee engagement. The persuasive manager maintains full control of the decision-making process but will spend a considerable amount of time trying to convince work groups of the benefits of the decisions and allaying any concerns they may have. The style excludes staff from the decision-making process. It enables decisions to be made quickly and provides employees with a full understanding of the background to the decision and how it is likely to affect their day-to-day jobs. On the negative side, use of the style is not guaranteed to gain employee support for the decisions. More importantly, such an approach fails to capitalize on the valuable views of those delivering the work on the front line. The adoption of this style could lead to lack of initiative and a fall in productivity due to resentment from people with no power over the decisions that are affecting them. This management style may be appropriate in difficult and challenging situations or when it is necessary to drive forward change to which the workforce is resistant.

Laissez-faire

A laissez-faire manager leaves staff to get on with their work with little interference. This sort of people manager tends to act as a mentor and stimulator. They rarely get involved in the detail and delivery of work objectives, preferring to work at a distance, engaging with people as necessary to offer them encouragement. These managers are known to be complete delegators of work on the basis of their view that employees are more motivated and committed if they feel they have full control and responsibility. This people management style is only really effective in teams that are made up of strong and competent members who need little guidance and minimal developmental support. They will feel trusted and empowered by the laissez-faire manager. It is most suitable for use in creative and entrepreneurial companies or teams made up of highly qualified professionals. There are clear risks to this type of management style, which lacks focus and direction and avoids involvement in day-to-day work.

Management by walking around (MBWA)

People managers who manage through walking around among team members and others within the organization are usually good listeners and use the information they gather from conversations to minimize challenges and avoid possible crises. They recognize that formal communication processes do not necessarily capture workers' concerns and suggestions or maintain morale. The MBWA manager can act upon the information obtained or use it to inform decision-making higher up the management chain. These managers act as coaches and counsellors. They are not necessarily involved in controlling and delivering the work objectives, and leave decision-making to the workers. There are risks around the loss of authority for those who adopt this type of management style, although it can lead to quick response times.

Paternalistic

Paternalistic people managers are generally regarded as managers who care about the people for whom they are responsible in a way that aims to achieve a balance between management decision-making and the well-being of employees. They are the sort of managers who take account of the impact of business decisions on the staff. Even though they may take decisions without involving others in the same way as an autocratic manager, their internal decision-making process analyses and takes account of the implications of those decisions on the workforce and strives to ensure their welfare is safeguarded. This management style of caring for others helps motivate workers, increases their loyalty and minimizes staff turnover. The downside is that it can create high dependency on the manager and if he or she makes an error or makes the wrong decision, staff may feel let down. There is also potential for dissent in the work group.

Summary of management styles

A management style incorporates your people management skills and provides a framework for decision-making, taking action and controlling work groups. We each have a natural management style that reflects who we are and our personal characteristics and behaviours. This may or may not be suitable for many of the situations you are faced with as a people manager. Your management style can be developed and adapted by improving your understanding of yourself and how you respond to certain individuals and people. Below is a table summarizing the features of the management styles we have discussed today together with their advantages and disadvantages.

Management style	Features	Advantages	Disadvantages
Autocratic	Unilateral decision-making Clear instructions	Rapid decisions Perception of strong and competent management	Employees feel disempowered and not trusted Fosters dependency and resentment Creates divisions between managers and workers
Democratic	Involvement of workers in decision-making	Staff ownership of decisions Improved job satisfaction and work quality Team-building Cooperation and good two-way communication between management and staff Creates culture for ideas to come forward	Lengthy decision-making process Decisions may not be in the business's interests Workers may not have the necessary skills and experience to make sound business decisions

Bureaucratic	Established rules and procedures to follow	Inspires confidence of stakeholders Reliable decision-making Mitigates business risks	Slow decision-making Demotivating for staff Costly
Consultative	Top down communication and decision-making Consultation with employees	Maintains morale of staff Could gain the commitment of workers	Staff feel disempowered
Persuasive	Unilateral decision-making Time spent allaying work group's concerns	Quick decision-making Staff provided with full information on the implications of decisions	Staff feel excluded from decision-making Fall in productivity Lack of initiative among the workers
Laissez-faire	Staff left to make decisions Complete delegation of work Manager at a distance, uninterested and hands-off	Competent and skilled staff could feel empowered and trusted	Lack of focus and direction Resentful staff
MBWA (management by walking around)	Good listening Visible and accessible manager Manager acts as coach and counsellor	Useful informal information is gathered Quick responses to issues Helps ward off any crises or prepare for any forthcoming challenges	Loss of authority and respect Reliance on team to deliver with limited direction and control
Paternalistic	Communication is downwards Decisions are autocratic Account is taken of the personal and social needs of the group	Staff involved in decisions, which could result in high morale Staff turnover low Employee loyalty	High dependency on manager Slows decision-making process If manager makes wrong decision, staff can become disenchanted and dissatisfied

Summary

An organization's success or failure can be influenced significantly by the people manager's style of managing. Your choice of management style, therefore, is likely to impact greatly on the performance of your staff.

The type of management style you choose to employ will usually reflect your personal characteristics.

As we have illustrated, each management style has its own pros and cons. A good people manager will be aware of his or her propensity to adopt one particular style and the benefits and disadvantages of using this in certain situations. Effective people managers will adapt their management approaches both to the individuals and the situations they face. It has been shown that there are significant benefits to be gained from adopting a people management style that involves listening, talking, supporting and working with your team on work objectives.

SUNDAY
MONDAY
TUESDAY
WEDNESDAY
THURSDAY
FRIDAY
SATURDAY

Fact-check (answers at the back)

1. In times of crisis, which management style should be used?
   a) Bureaucratic ☐
   b) Persuasive ☐
   c) MBWA ☐
   d) Autocratic ☐

2. A disadvantage of the democratic style is:
   a) Can lead to conflict ☐
   b) Resistance to decisions ☐
   c) Could result in poor decisions ☐
   d) Staff resentment ☐

3. The bureaucratic style is appropriate for:
   a) Creative organizations ☐
   b) Times of crisis ☐
   c) Regulated businesses ☐
   d) Team building ☐

4. Quick decisions require:
   a) A laissez-faire style ☐
   b) Autocratic management ☐
   c) MBWA ☐
   d) Staff involvement ☐

5. Which management style leads to sound decision-making?
   a) Paternalistic ☐
   b) MBWA ☐
   c) Bureaucratic ☐
   d) Consultative ☐

6. A consultative manager:
   a) Involves staff in decisions ☐
   b) Decides unilaterally ☐
   c) Lets staff decide ☐
   d) Takes the majority view ☐

7. The advantage of MBWA is:
   a) Quick decisions ☐
   b) Prepared for threats ☐
   c) Involves staff ☐
   d) Clear direction ☐

8. A disadvantage of paternalistic management is:
   a) Over-reliance on the manager ☐
   b) Employee uninterest ☐
   c) Creates conflict ☐
   d) Loss of commitment ☐

9. Which management style involves unilateral decision-making?
   a) Laissez-faire ☐
   b) Persuasive ☐
   c) Democratic ☐
   d) Bureaucratic ☐

10. Which management style is suitable for creative workers?
    a) Autocratic ☐
    b) Paternalistic ☐
    c) Laissez-faire ☐
    d) MBWA ☐

THURSDAY

Tools for people management

Over the past four days we have covered what is meant by people management, the role of people managers, motivational theories and the features of various people management styles together with their advantages and disadvantages. It is now time to focus on tools to support you in your task of managing people.

There are numerous tools available which primarily relate to people management, performance management, quality management, strategy development, project management, process and organizational change, and environmental management. Some of these are linked to accreditation processes, to which we will refer briefly.

Today we are going to discuss the basic aspects of the main tools that a people manager can access under the management components listed above. Some of these are inter-related, such as people and performance management.

You will gain a knowledge of:

The main tools that are available to support you in becoming an effective people manager

How these tools will improve the overall performance of your team, and your credibility and reputation within the business

Management tools and techniques

People managers develop primarily through learning on the job. However, there are numerous tools and techniques available to help them deal with particular issues or develop certain areas within the work group. These can be useful for developing people, managing change, developing strategies and plans, managing projects, delivering quality-assured goods and services, and ensuring good environmental management.

People development tools

A people manager can access a number of psychometric tests to inform him or her on how a staff member should be motivated and managed, and the role he or she should play in the work group in order to benefit the team and the business as a whole. These tests are also useful for assessing development areas and deciding how these should be tackled. We will be discussing the training and development of people on Saturday, but today we are going to explore how the knowledge of psychometric testing can help in this respect.

There are two types of psychometric tests: those which assess an individual's numerical, verbal or reasoning ability, frequently referred to as aptitude tests; and those which focus on personality to uncover a person's preferred style of behaviour or motivation. You may wish to use psychometric tests in relation to recruitment for vacancies in the team, to inform coaching sessions, for team building or for career development purposes. There are many testing tools available so the people manager needs to be clear about what is needed from the test in order to select the most relevant type.

Numerical, verbal and reasoning tests are helpful in assessing the particular aptitudes, abilities and intelligence of candidates for employment or promotion. There are a wide range of tests available which, in effect, are structured, systematic ways of assessing a person's numerical, logical and verbal reasoning. They are usually used as part of the overall assessment process for recruitment or promotion. These tests are administered under examination conditions and can involve solving problems, undertaking tasks or answering multiple-choice questions. The most common form of tests are:

Test	Method and ability assessed
Numerical reasoning	A number of arithmetical problems and mathematical questions, possibly presented in charts and graphs that need interpretation. These are used to assess people's ability to handle and interpret numbers.
Logical reasoning	These tests expect the candidate to identify rules and patterns from information provided in diagram sequences containing various shapes in order to find the next one in the sequence. The ability to think logically and analytically is tested.
Non-verbal reasoning	Diagrams and pictures are used to assess the candidate's capability of analysing and solving problems through this means.
Verbal reasoning	This type of test consists of a number of relatively short paragraphs of written text, from which the candidate is expected to assess the accuracy of a number of statements based on the information. It is used to assess abilities in understanding, analysing and interpreting complex written information.
Verbal logic	Verbal logic tests involve solving a number of puzzles of different types. They test ability to think logically, analytically and numerically, and extract meaning from complex information.

Personality tests are very useful for people managers to understand their own behaviours, motivations and empathy, as well as those within the work group. Understanding your personality and that of others is fundamental to motivating teams in order to capitalize on their strengths and needs. People are all different and information from personality tests helps build appreciation of individuals' values and special strengths and qualities, along with understanding of their behaviour traits.

A number of personality tests are based on the theories of the psychologist Carl Jung, who developed concepts of psychological types. He identified two types of attitudes in humans i.e. introverted and extroverted. The latter tends to be objective and outwards focused, while the former is subjective and inwardly motivated. It is acknowledged that both characteristics are present in everyone to varying degrees and that many people have a healthy balance of the two aspects.

Jung developed a framework of four functional types which he related to extroversion and introversion. These were thinking and feeling, which enable the taking of decisions and forming of judgements rationally because they reason, decide and make judgements; and sensation and intuition, which are irrational acts based on the gathering of information and perceptions. On this basis, Jung developed eight personality types, from which the popular Myers Briggs personality test, known as MBTI (Myers Briggs Type Indicator), was developed. This test is widely used for understanding and interpreting personality and preferred ways of behaving in the workplace. It is useful for:

- understanding and developing yourself and others
- understanding what motivates others
- understanding others' strengths and weaknesses
- building effective teams
- allocating tasks and responsibilities
- agreeing roles within a work group
- identifying your own and others' development needs.

More recently, a psychologist named Eysenck developed a test that measures personality on the two scales of:

- introversion–extraversion
- stability–instability (unemotional–emotional).

His tests provide a valuable additional perspective to the work of previous psychologists by assessing through detailed questioning whether individuals' temperaments are stable or not and whether they fall within the introversion or extroversion category. His theory produces four main types of personality.

Stable extrovert (unemotional extrovert)	Stable introvert (unemotional introvert)
Sociable, outgoing, talkative, responsive, easy-going, lively, carefree leadership	Calm, even-tempered, reliable, controlled, peaceful, thoughtful, careful, passive
Unstable introvert (emotional introvert)	Unstable extrovert (emotional extrovert)
Moody, anxious, rigid, sober, pessimistic, reserved, unsociable, quiet	Touchy, aggressive, excitable, changeable, impulsive, optimistic, active

People can display a mixture of these characteristics. As a people manager it is helpful to use this model to understand your own and others' personality types.

The US company Inscape developed a system known as the DISC model, which is frequently used for organizational development purposes. It is based on the assumption that the foundation of personal and professional success lies in knowing yourself, understanding others and realizing the impact of your action and behaviours on others. The method assesses Dominance, Influence, Steadiness and Compliance (DISC). Dominance and compliance relate to things, and influence and steadiness to people. The model provides a personality description based on determination of a person's dominant preferred style and supporting styles.

A well-used team building assessment tool is Belbin's team roles based on the research undertaken by Dr Meredith Belbin. This has shown that teams balanced with people of different but complementary competencies perform more effectively than less well-balanced teams. This model is used by many of the UK's top companies and a significant number internationally. A set of nine team roles have been identified, including a specialist role. The particular strengths, styles and functions associated with the roles are specified as:

Role name	Strengths and styles	Functions and tasks
Coordinator	Confident, mature with ability to motivate everyone to achieve shared goals	Clarifies group objectives, sets agendas, establishes priorities, identifies problems, sums up and is decisive, does not dominate discussions
Shaper	Energetic, assertive, competitive, motivated, achievement driven	Shapes the team's efforts, looks for patterns in discussions and identifies practical considerations. Gets results. Can steam-roller the team
Planter	Creative, unorthodox, innovative, inventive, imaginative, problem-solving	Source of original ideas, puts forward radical, original ideas, suggestions and proposals
Monitor-evaluator	Analytical, prudent, serious, critical thinker	Provides a measured and dispassionate analysis through objectivity. Stops the team being committed to a misguided task
Implementer	Reliable, loyal, structured, systematic, practical, dependable, efficient	Turns decisions and strategies into defined and measurable tasks, sorting out objectives and pursuing them logically.

Resource investigator	Good communicator, networker, outgoing, affable. Quick, negotiator, seeks and finds options	Brings in ideas, information and developments from outside the team. Salesperson, diplomat, liaison officer and explorer
Team worker	Supportive, sociable, flexible, adaptable, perceptive, listener, calming influence, mediator	Operates against division and disruption in the team, cements members together in times of stress and pressure
Completer-finisher	Accurate, attention to detail, high standards, quality-orientated, delivers to schedule and specification	Maintains a sense of urgency with relentless follow-through
Specialist	Technical expert, highly focused capability and knowledge driven by professional standards and dedication to subject area	Contributes detailed technical and specialist advice

The roles of coordinator, shaper, planter and resource investigator are noted as requiring extrovert tendencies. In small teams people frequently assume more than one role. The method is useful in helping teams improve their behaviours and performance when issues such as conflict, failure to meet targets or continual mistakes arise. In such circumstances it would be necessary to assess whether the team has the right skills in terms of coordinators, resource investigators and evaluators. The interaction between different personalities within a team leads to conflict on occasions so applying the Belbin model can assist each team member to understand and value their differences.

Another well-used personality test is the 'Big Five' factors. This trait theory has been fully researched by a number of psychologists. It measures traits by scoring them on the following scales:

- Extroversion versus Introversion
- Confidence versus Sensitive

- Detail-conscious versus Unstructured
- Tough-minded versus Agreeable
- Conforming versus Creative.

The higher the score, the more likely the candidate will be to exhibit the behaviour and the less able to show behaviours at the lower end of the scale. The factors need to be combined to indicate how people operate and their underlying preferences. The five factor model is best used to assess non-managerial staff. It is quick to use and provides accurate results. It is effective at enabling an understanding of someone's key drivers. There are a number of other personality tests that are closely linked to the Big Five factors. These include Belbin's team roles and others known as 16PF, Occupational Personality Questionnaire (OPQ), Fundamental Interpersonal Relations Orientation–Behaviour (Firo–B), the Birkman method and the Lumina Spark system.

People managers should have a basic understanding of a number of personality tests and assessment tools such as these so that they can consider their use in particular situations. Tests are useful for building self-awareness, personal development, motivation, training, selection and recruitment, and people management. They help the people manager understand team members and manage communications, relationships and behaviours more effectively. They are a valuable aid to motivation and management.

Strategic development tools

Every business needs to scan the external environment and look ahead for planning purposes in order to remain competitive and survive. The two most widely used tools for deciding the strategic directions of a business are known as PEST and SWOT analyses.

PEST is an acronym for Political, Economic, Social and Technological factors. Generally, it is used in a marketing context. It encourages more lateral thinking. PEST provides a framework for looking at situations, reviewing and updating strategies or plans, establishing direction, considering a marketing proposition or assessing whether a new product or service is likely to be viable. The model is sometimes expanded to include legal and environmental factors (PESTLE). In use, appropriate questions or prompts are developed for the market issue under consideration. These are aligned to the four PEST quadrants. The issue needs to be clearly defined so that those contributing to the exercise understand fully the purpose and implications of the PEST model. In carrying out the PEST analysis, you can score the issues listed in each section. This is particularly useful if you are comparing more than one option for market entry purposes or business development opportunities. An example of the model to be followed is given here.

Subject (e.g. market, business proposition etc.)	
Political Current legislative framework Planned legislation Government and regional policies International situation Trading conditions Grants available Pressure or campaigning groups Environmental issues	**Economic** Current domestic economic situation Economic forecasts International economic outlook Taxation issues Seasonal and climate impacts Market cycles Specific sector outlook Interest and other bank charges Exchange rates International trade implications
Social Demographics Social trends Consumer attitudes, opinions and buying habits Brand image Product trends Media coverage Selling channels Diversity PR and advertising Ethical issues	**Technological** Technology developments Research and its funding Dependent technologies Technology solutions Production capacity Information and communications technology Consumer use of technology Innovation Licensing and patents Intellectual property Global technological issues

Note: the issues listed are given solely as a guide.

SWOT is an acronym for analysing the Strengths, Weaknesses, Opportunities and Threats for assessment of a business or proposition. It follows on from a PEST analysis, which provides you with market assessments from the standpoint of a particular proposition or business. SWOT assesses the strength of a business or proposition in the context of its competitors. The analysis is carried out under the headings of strengths, weaknesses, opportunities and threats, and the factors that appear in each of these quadrants are similar to those given above for the PEST assessment.

Finally, it is worth touching upon the concept of the Balanced Score Card, which has been defined as 'a strategic planning and management system used to align business activities to the vision statement of an organization'. Alternatively, it can be viewed as an attempt to embed an organization's vision and mission statements into practical implementation across the whole business. The Balanced Score Card is aimed at improving efficiency and joining up the interdependent, internal operations in relation to finance, internal processes, learning and development, and customers or clients. Prior to developing the score card you need to be aware of the business's vision, mission and strategic plan, and know its financial situation, its structure and operating procedures, employees' skill levels, customer satisfaction levels and other areas that may be identified for improvement. The following is an example of the areas that could possibly be improved under these headings.

Department	Areas
Finance	Return on investment Cash flow Return on capital employed Profit levels and other financial results
Internal business processed	Number of activities for each function Duplicate activities across functions Allocation of processes to the right department Blockages and delays in processes Computerization of processes

Learning and development	Appropriateness of employee skills levels
	Employee turnover
	Sickness absences
	Job satisfaction
	Training and development
Customers/clients	Delivery performance
	Quality performance
	Customer satisfaction
	Complaints/returns
	Percentage of market
	Retention rates

Measurements need to be set for each of these factors which are SMART (see the Monday chapter) and clearly aligned with the organization's strategic plan. The process can lead to more effective and relevant information systems, efficient processes, highly motivated and skilled employees, improved financial management and greater customer satisfaction.

Decision-making tools

All people managers have to solve problems and make decisions. These are closely linked tasks and there are systems available to improve the quality of your decision-making. The strategic development tools above can help in decision-making, but brainstorming is also another way of solving problems and making decisions. It is effective at unleashing creativity and identifying options. Workshops can also be useful for taking major decisions that require the commitment and support of all staff. A simple, straightforward method is to write down the pros and cons of particular options. This involves assessing the advantages and disadvantages, the points in favour and those against.

The steps to be followed for solving problems and taking decisions are:

● define and clarify the issue
● collect all the facts and build up an understanding of the reasons for the problem
● consider all possible options and solutions
● analyse the advantages and disadvantages of each option

- select the best option and make the decision
- explain your decision to those affected and ensure effective implementation.

This method, which can be scored, is best applied to routine decisions that are unlikely to have a major impact on the business. For example, buying a relatively inexpensive new piece of equipment or travelling to a meeting. A scored example is:

Should I travel to a meeting or handle the matter by video-conferencing?			
Pros (for – advantages)	Score	Cons (against – disadvantages)	Score
Face-to-face contact	3	Cost and time involved	5
Opportunity to build relationships	3	Difficult issues may be raised	3
Could visit other suppliers in the area	3	Not available to manage staff	4
Ability to assess operations on site	2		
Total: 4 pros	11	Total: 3 cons	12

When decisions involve a number of options and choices, the brainstorming method can be the most effective option. This is also suitable for use in a workshop setting. The method identifies and helps solve problems by developing decision-making options. It is suitable for use when there are more than a couple of options available and the decision is likely to have a relatively high impact on the business, for example selection of a new site for location of the business or deciding on new markets.

The process is:

- identify options and on a sheet for each, write the option concerned together with a pros and cons column
- write down as many impacts and implications as possible in each of the columns
- weight these on scores of 1 to 3, or 1 to 5, with 1 being the lowest
- compare the total scores and choose the most attractive option.

Some people are natural decision-makers, others may be better at analysing problems. Regardless of whether you are good at decision-making or problem analysis, these tools should help you and your team improve your decision-making capability and the quality of those decisions.

Quality management tools

All people managers need to be concerned about the quality of their staff, the work they undertake and the team's outputs. Quality management involves planning, control, assurance and improvement of a product or service. Processes are crucial to ensuring total quality management, which is defined as 'a set of coordinated activities to direct and control an organization in order to continually improve the effectiveness and efficiency of its performance'. A wide range of Total Quality Management tools are available to identify, measure, prioritize and improve processes. The best-known is probably the ISO 9000 standards; others include Kaizen, Six Sigma, EFQM and many more. It is likely that these will be organization-wide so as a people manager you will need to have a basic understanding of the concepts and the implications for you and your team.

Quality management is based primarily on the following eight principles, which form the basis of the ISO (International Organization for Standardization) 9000 quality management system.

- An understanding of the needs of current and future customers, and meeting or exceeding their expectations. The focus should be on both external and internal customers.
- Strong leadership which is directional and motivational, and creates and maintains an internal culture of quality improvement.
- Involvement of people at all levels of the organization to capitalize on their abilities for the benefit of the organization.
- Process approach bringing together activities and related resources.
- All inter-related process are identified, understood and managed as a system in order to achieve quality objectives to contribute to the organization's efficiency and effectiveness.
- Continual improvement of overall performance.
- Decisions are based on facts from analysis of data and other information.
- Mutually beneficial supplier relationships in order to add value.

ISO 9000 quality management standards are aimed at delivering performance improvement through certifying an organization's processes and systems. One of the criticisms of it is that it is not concerned with the quality of the product or service.

Kaizen originated in Japan, where total quality management was pioneered. The word means continuous improvement. It is a way of thinking, working and behaving in accordance with the values and culture of an organization with the aims of being:

- profitable, stable, sustainable and innovative
- focused on eliminating waste and increasing productivity
- proactive in identifying potential problems in systems, processes and activities, and rectifying them before they arise
- creative in establishing a harmonious and dynamic organization in which everyone participates and is valued for their contribution.

It involves every aspect of the business all the time as well as full participation and empowerment of everyone. It uses a range of analytical tools and techniques to review systems and improve processes. There are close connections between the Kaizen philosophy and those of motivational theorists such as Maslow, Herzberg and McGregor, covered on Tuesday.

Six Sigma is suitable primarily for large manufacturing enterprises, but more recently has been applied to the service industry. It aims to improve the quality of process outputs by identifying and eradicating the causes of any defects or errors. It relies on statistical information and experts. The process involves a defined order of steps to be taken and has quantified financial targets aimed at cost reductions and/or increased profits. Recently the system has been developed in the light of lean manufacturing ideas to create the methodology known as Lean Six Sigma which aims for business and operational excellence by combining a focus on process flow and waste issues with the original Six Sigma focus on variation and design.

There is some debate about the effectiveness of Six Sigma in securing tangible business growth. Some regard it as no more than a basic quality improvement system that does not give rise to new products or technological innovation and which stifles creativity and innovation. Another criticism is its attention to reducing variation rather than robustness of systems to eliminate any need to reduce variation.

The **EFQM** (European Foundation for Quality Management) Excellence Model is a management framework which takes a holistic view of an organization. It is suitable for use in organizations of all sizes and from all sectors. It is widely used in both public and private sector organizations. The model is a self-assessment tool which uses nine criteria for identification and analysis of a body's strengths and weaker areas in order to develop an improvement plan aimed at sustainable growth and enhanced performance. The nine criteria are:

Enablers
1 Leadership
2 Strategy
3 People
4 Partnerships and resources
5 Process, products and service

Results
6 Key results
7 People results
8 Society results
9 Customer results

The first five criteria are regarded as 'enablers' because they cover what is done and how, while the remaining four are classified as 'results' because they are focused on what an organization achieves or delivers.

The model is based on the following eight Fundamental Concepts of Excellence.

1 Achieving balanced results

Excellent organizations meet their mission and progress towards their vision through planning and achieving a balanced set of results that meet both the short- and long-term needs of their stakeholders and, where relevant, exceed them.

2 Adding value for customers

Excellent organizations know that customers are their primary reason for being and strive to innovate and create value for them by understanding and anticipating their needs and expectations.

3 Leading with vision, inspiration and integrity

Excellent organizations have leaders who shape the future and make it happen, acting as role models for its values and ethics.

4 Managing by processes

Excellent organizations are managed through structured and strategically aligned processes using fact-based decision-making to create balanced and sustained results.

5 Succeeding through people

Excellent organizations value their people and create a culture of empowerment for the balanced achievement of organizational and personal goals.

6 Nurturing creativity and innovation

Excellent organizations generate increased value and levels of performance through continual and systematic innovation by harnessing the creativity of their stakeholders.

7 Building partnerships

Excellent organizations seek, develop and maintain trusting relationships with various partners to ensure mutual success. These partnerships may be formed with customers, society, key suppliers, educational bodies or non-governmental organizations (NGOs).

8 Taking responsibility for a sustainable future

Excellent organizations embed within their culture an ethical mindset, clear values and the highest standards of organizational behaviour, all of which enable them to strive for economic, social and ecological sustainability.

Although there is evidence of the success of organizations that have implemented the EFQM model in respect of both performance and outputs, it has been criticized for not supporting the remedying of problems. There is also a view that the model is best suited to transactional environments.

Project management tools

Project management tools can be useful for the people manager in a number of situations. They are primarily used for planning and managing change, but can be applied to a number of tasks, projects of all sizes and in a number of functional areas, including people management. A similar process is followed for all projects.

- Agree the specification (terms of reference) for the project.
- Plan implementation in terms of timescale, financial and staff resources, and milestones.
- Communicate to those involved and all those with an interest.
- Agree and allocate project actions.
- Manage the project through communicating, encouraging and enabling team members.
- Monitor implementation, review progress, adjust plans as necessary and communicate.

- Complete, review and report on performance.
- Follow up to ensure effective implementation through training, support and reporting of benefits.

The specification, or terms of reference, should provide a clear and accurate description of the project aims and generally cover its background, objectives, scope, constraints, assumptions, reporting and management arrangements, dependencies, estimates and timescales. The various stages of the project should be carefully planned, involving the team wherever possible. There are a number of tools available for detailed project planning which are relatively easy to understand. An example is a Gantt chart, which presents a separate timeline for each component part of the project, detailing the activity and costs. Another example is a Critical Path Analysis flow diagram, a linear flow diagram of the timeline that shows the anticipated timing of the use of resources and when activities will be carried out. The latter illustrates what needs to be done and when.

Most projects involving expenditure will require a spreadsheet such as MS Excel for planning, monitoring and reporting expenditure. Project timescales and costs should be realistic and not overambitious, and some risk assessment should be undertaken, including planning for contingencies. As regards the project team, this should be made up of committed individuals with the relevant skills and experience. Communication within the team and to relevant interests is vital in order to keep everyone informed and to secure their support, agreement and cooperation. The project activities delegated to the relevant team member need to be clear and accord with the SMART concept (see the Monday chapter).

Managing the project and motivating the team requires the people management approach we are covering this week, in particular what we learnt about managerial roles on Monday, and motivation and management styles on Tuesday and Wednesday. Once the project is completed, a review and report is necessary, together with follow-up, which may involve training and change management.

Project management is a specialized area of management, in a similar way to quality management, so it is not necessary for you, as a people manager, to have in-depth knowledge of the various techniques unless you are leading or are closely involved in a major project. Apart from Gantt charts and Critical Path Analysis, there are numerous software packages for project management purposes. In day-to-day work as a people manager, you will usually only need to apply the principles of project management.

Environmental management tools

Environmental management is likely to be an organization-wide function. As a people manager you would not normally be involved in detailed implementation unless you work in the functional area. However, all managers need to have an understanding of the environmental management tools and techniques used in their organization as they will be expected to ensure that their teams comply with the necessary requirements. With the increasing emphasis on the environmental impact of businesses of all types, organizations are now becoming aware of their responsibilities in relation to environmental sustainability. The best-known environmental management models and processes are EMS (Environmental Management Systems), ISO 14001 and EMAS (the Eco-management and Audit Scheme).

EMS is a comprehensive, systematic, planned and documented way of managing an organization's environmental policy and improving its environmental performance. It covers the organizational structure together with planning and resource allocation for developing and implementing environmental programmes to minimize the impact of an organization's whole range of activities on the environment. EMS is concerned with evaluations of practices, processes and procedures with a focus on continual improvement. The model follows a Plan-Do-Check-Act (PDCA) cycle.

ISO (International Organization for Standardization) 14001 is an environmental management standard which sets out the specific standards to be met in order for an organization to be certified. It has been adopted globally. EMS may incorporate ISO 14001, the aim of which is to improve environmental performance and legal compliance across a range of relevant aspects in order to save costs through waste minimization and efficient use of energy and water, ensure compliance with environmental regulation and manage risks effectively.

The Eco-Management and Audit Scheme (EMAS) is a European Union voluntary certification scheme which incorporates ISO 14001 but is more comprehensive and robust. It demands strict adherence to the measurement and evaluation of environmental performance targets against set targets in relation to six environmental indicators. These indicators cover efficiency in the use of energy, materials, waste and emissions as well as protection of biodiversity. The system has been shown to lead to significant business cost savings.

Summary

Today we have covered briefly the various tools that are available to you as a people manager to support you in managing the performance of your staff, developing or contributing to strategy formulation, project managing tasks and understanding quality and environmental management systems. These tools can be useful in enabling you to become more effective in your role as a people manager.

People management is a highly variable role. It is impossible to be prescriptive about how to carry out the task because of its many variables. Knowledge of people management, strategy development, project management, and environmental and quality management tools and techniques should contribute to your efficiency and effectiveness in your multifarious people management tasks.

SUNDAY
MONDAY
TUESDAY
WEDNESDAY
THURSDAY
FRIDAY
SATURDAY

Fact-check (answers at the back)

1. People's aptitudes can be tested through:
   a) SWOT ❏
   b) EMAS ❏
   c) Verbal reasoning ❏
   d) MBTI ❏

2. Team-working roles are established through:
   a) ISO 14001 ❏
   b) Belbin ❏
   c) Brain-storming ❏
   d) Logical reasoning ❏

3. Psychometric tests are used for:
   a) Decision-making ❏
   b) Recruitment ❏
   c) Planning ❏
   d) Market assessment ❏

4. Which of the following is one of Belbin's team role names?
   a) Coordinator ❏
   b) Leader ❏
   c) Strategist ❏
   d) Manager ❏

5. Firo–B is a type of:
   a) Strategic tool ❏
   b) Environmental system ❏
   c) Personality test ❏
   d) Decision-making tool ❏

6. PEST means...
   Complete the words.
   a) P...... ❏
   b) E...... ❏
   c) S...... ❏
   d) T...... ❏

7. SWOT is used for:
   a) Market assessment ❏
   b) Decision-making ❏
   c) Strategic planning ❏
   d) Quality management ❏

8. The Balanced Score Card is used for:
   a) Project management ❏
   b) Environmental management ❏
   c) Decision-making ❏
   d) Strategic planning ❏

9. EFQM is a:
   a) Environmental system ❏
   b) Quality management system ❏
   c) Project management system ❏
   d) Decision-making system ❏

10. A Gantt chart is a tool for:
    a) Personality assessment ❏
    b) Team-building ❏
    c) Project management ❏
    d) Strategic planning ❏

FRIDAY

How people managers manage performance

We should now have a sound understanding of people management, what people managers do, how to motivate staff, people managers' various management styles, and the tools and techniques that are available to people managers to help them do their jobs. Today it is time to look at how people managers can performance manage their teams effectively in the wider organizational context.

We are going to discuss the meaning of performance management and how this is done in practice. A sample work plan aimed at improvement is provided as an illustration of how you can compile a plan for your team in order to monitor and review performance against targets and objectives on a regular basis.

We cover the performance management process and the performance management tools that are available at organizational, team and individual levels. Finally, we conclude by summarizing the benefits of effective performance management.

By the end of today you should have developed:

an understanding of performance management

an understanding of how to implement it in practice

Performance management

Performance management is a process at the heart of people management. It is about ensuring that the goals of the organization, division, team or unit and individuals are realized in the most effective and efficient manner. In effect, it takes place at all of these levels. Effective performance management is dependent on having the right systems and people in place. It needs to be integrated into day-to-day management tasks. Generally, all businesses of a reasonable size have a strategic plan underpinned with annual business plans, which are reviewed throughout the year. On Thursday we covered performance management tools that relate to the implementation of these plans and are suitable for use at organizational, divisional and team level, such as EFQM, Six Sigma and the Balanced Score Card.

Performance management should take a long-term view of the development of teams and individuals in line with business requirements. It needs a structure which provides a framework to enable people to understand what is required of them. The corporate strategic goals are a starting point from which departmental and team performance and development goals can be developed into a work plan suitable for regular review. In order to manage performance successfully at a team and individual level, the people manager needs to have a clear work plan covering the financial year which is linked to the overall organizational plan. It is important to have input into the plan from staff responsible for delivering the work objectives.

Performance management at all levels follows a cycle which involves planning, taking action, reviewing and revising. Each team or unit should have a delivery plan which relates to higher-level business plans and strategies. Team members should have had an opportunity to contribute to the plan and the individuals concerned should have an annual performance plan which sets out their expected contribution to the delivery of the plan. The individual performance plan is a tool for managing both someone's behaviour and outputs. It is aimed at developing people and improving their performance by aligning personal goals with those of the wider organization. A people manager can use performance management for maximizing the performance of the team or individual or to deal with poor performance. Although the principles are the same, the former is often a more collaborative, informal process, while the latter involves confronting performance issues and recording formally the steps in the process because it can lead to disciplinary proceedings or termination of employment.

In performance managing staff, a people manager should ensure that individuals understand clearly what is expected of them in terms of output, contributions, behaviours and development. You should also ensure that people have the necessary knowledge, skills and abilities to deliver; if these are deficient in any way, provide support to address any knowledge or skills gaps or any behavioural issues. Sensitive feedback is an important part of this, which should be a two-way conversation so there is understanding and clarification of perspectives and perceptions. It provides an opportunity for staff to communicate their needs and wishes regarding how they are managed. People managers need to be aware of the impact of their own behaviour on others and be concerned to demonstrate positive behaviours.

Performance management is, therefore, a two-way process for developing successful relationships between the people manager and the individual as well as the team. It is a continuous process which covers all aspects relevant to running a successful business and forms part of day-to-day management. Successful people management is dependent on effective performance management, which brings together people with systems and processes in an environment shaped by leadership and culture.

The right organizational culture is critical to improving performance management. It is difficult to describe a culture. It is best explained as the sum total of the beliefs, values and behaviours of individuals within a given group. An organizational culture is the means by which norms of acceptable behaviour are established, although it is not

Example of a team performance plan

Organizational aim: To increase the levels of manufacture and sales of high-value cheeses by 20%						
Divisional aim: To market a range of high-value cheeses and increase sales by 20%						
Team aim: To market the cheeses and increase the number of customers leading to 20% increase in sales Staff resources: 1 marketing manager (MM), 1 assistant marketing manager (AMM) and 2 marketing assistants (MA) Financial resource: £1 million						
Objective	**Tasks**	**Staff resource**	**Financial resource**	**Milestone**	**Target**	**Outcomes**
To develop a marketing campaign	Undertake market research Market segmentation Prepare marketing plan	MM 0.2 AMM 0.3 MA 0.5	£50,000	05 April 12 April 25 April	30 April	Agreed marketing plan for implementation
To attend trade and consumer shows in order to increase customer base by 20%	Identify appropriate show Make booking Organize stands and staffing arrangements Attend shows Follow up actions	MM 0.4 AMM 0.2 MA 0.5	£250,000	14 April 30 April 6 weeks before show On show days Within 5 days	4 shows annually	£1.5m of new orders 20 new customers

Objective	Task	Resources	Budget	Timing	Target	Success measure
To organize advertising campaign in order to generate new leads	Commission agency	MM 0.2	£500,000	30 April	Peak viewing figures	Two campaigns generating 50 new leads
	Agree advertisement copy etc	AMM 0.3		31 May	1,000 social media mentions	
	Approve campaign	MA 0.5		30 June		
	Monitor implementation			Ongoing		
To organize PR to create greater brand awareness	Draft and issue press releases	MM 0.2	£200,000	Minimum of 1 a week	15 annually	Increase in media coverage
	Updating of website	AMM 0.2		Daily	Up-to-date website	Increase in website hits
	Twitter comments and monitoring	MA 0.5		Daily	Daily comment	Increase in Twitter comments
	Facebook updates and monitoring			Daily	Daily update	Increase in number of Facebook hits

Note: on average an employee works for about 44 weeks a year (220 days). One day of a five-day working week is 0.2 days, half a day is 0.1.

unusual in larger organizations to have a number of sub-cultures. In some organizations a culture of performance improvement may exist where the ethos of continual improvement is embedded among all staff who are keen to provide the best possible products/services to its customers and clients. In others, a performance management culture is found where the emphasis is on management through the development of systems and processes to measure and report on performance with the aim of improvement.

Managing performance requires the striking of a balance between nurturing and developing people and ensuring that the team's goals and objectives are achieved, and that a valuable contribution is made to the overall performance of the business. A people manager has to achieve this balance according to the particular situation they face and doing so is challenging. For example, a people manager may be under pressure to deliver work objectives for which he or she is accountable, but this is affected by a key member of staff underperforming due to personal circumstances outside the control of the people manager. The people manager will need to assess many such challenging situations and adopt the most appropriate managerial response as there is an inextricable link between good people management and good performance.

The performance management process

The role of the people manager in relationship to performance management is to show leadership and be an exemplar in terms of his or her performance and behaviour. Through his or her own performance the people manager should achieve the following.

● **Set out a clear vision for the team's performance in line with the wider organizational goals and culture.**
Individuals need to know how their work fits in with the rest of the business and how their contribution can make a difference to the business's success or failure.

- **Communicate to the team and individuals what is expected of them in terms of quality of work, quantity of work, timescales, milestones and behaviours.**

Poor or ineffective communication is frequently the reason why people fail to perform to the expected standards. People need to know, without doubt, what expectations there are of them and these expectations need to be reasonable in terms of the ability and capacity of the individual. It is always worthwhile seeking the agreement of staff to what is required of them.

- **Motivate staff and continually monitor performance.**

The importance of motivation of staff was covered on Tuesday and the role of the people manager in monitoring and controlling performance was discussed on Monday. It needs to be emphasized that people managers should support and help staff in meeting the standards and expectations the organization has of them. Seeking agreement to performance expectations provides an opportunity to explore with a staff member what help or support is needed. It is important to ask in order to test out perceptions and avoid presumptions. People need to know for certain what is to be done, why and how.

- **Engage staff in planning; seek and act upon their views on performance improvements.**

The people manager should work in harmony with team members. He or she should not normally act in isolation from the team, particularly in respect of work planning and performance improvement. Individual team members can make a valuable contribution to preparation of a challenging but achievable plan and are well-placed to suggest ways in which performance can be improved at individual and team levels.

- **Provide regular praise and feedback on areas for improvement.**

People need to know how they are performing. They value positive feedback and expressions of appreciation. Equally, they would prefer to have immediate feedback on areas for improvement, rather than be informed at a later date or not be told at all. Negative feedback should be delivered in a supportive and non-judgemental way, focused on an area referred to as less strong rather than as a weakness.

- **Support the performance and development of staff.**
  The majority of people will need support at some time. This may relate to help in completing a task because the timescale is too tight, clarification of a problem, the need for advice in dealing with a difficult customer, time off to deal with an unexpected domestic problem, and numerous other issues that crop up from time to time that may impact on a person's performance. It is part of the role of a people manager to support his or her staff in dealing with any difficulties that arise. We will touch upon people development in more detail on Saturday, but this is a good point to flag up that many people are keen to learn and develop. Some will become disenchanted with their jobs if they are not challenged, stretched and given development opportunities. The people manager needs to know his or her staff sufficiently well to understand their motivations and identify those that need continual development and those that need developmental support to carry out their jobs to a satisfactory standard.
- **Facilitate learning and development.**
  Following on from the above, businesses that have people learning and development embedded in their cultures are often the most successful. A people manager should identify staff who would benefit from learning and development initiatives and facilitate this through providing the time and/or financial resources to allow it to take place for the good of the individual and the benefit of the business.
- **Be a model of exemplary behaviour in terms of good performance management.**
  If you are respected as a people manager by demonstrating your commitment to excellent performance, showing empathy with team members and displaying ethical behaviours in accordance with the norms of the organization, people will want to emulate your commitment and behaviours. This will have a beneficial effect on the work and reputation of the business. Conversely, if you say the right words but do not act them out, people will soon note your lack of authenticity and will be less inclined to perform to the best of their ability.

Performance management tools

Performance appraisal

Performance appraisal, sometimes known as a
performance review or performance evaluation, is an
important component of performance management.
Performance management is a strategic, holistic process
which brings together all the activities that contribute
to the successful management of people and teams in
order to achieve high levels of performance. Performance
appraisal is one of a number of performance management
tools. It is focused on the individual and adopts a relatively
short-term approach. The process provides an opportunity
for the people manager to talk to individual team members
about their performance, development needs and the
extent of managerial support needed. It is about reviewing
past performance, identifying areas which have been
done well and those where improvement is needed. The
appraisal process also considers and agrees an individual's
development needs.

Performance appraisal is another tool for people managers
to use to successfully manage their teams, with a focus on
improvement, development and behavioural management.
An individual performance plan should, therefore, cover the
many aspects of successful people management such as
goal achievements and behaviours, as well as learning and
development.

The people manager carries out the appraisal process,
which should be concerned with an individual's overall job
performance, in particular the quality of their work and
their outputs in line with pre-agreed criteria and targets.
The exercise is usually carried out annually, but it is
advisable to undertake mid-year reviews. Its main purpose
is performance improvement, but it can serve the purposes
of identification of talent, disciplinary action, termination of
employment and application of pay and reward systems, and
provides the opportunity for one-to-one communication.

Generally, performance appraisal follows six steps.

1 Measurement of performance against previously agreed targets and objectives, which should correlate with the team's work plan – an example of which has been given earlier in this chapter.
2 Evaluation of behaviours and attitudes against the organization's espoused values.
3 Positive feedback in terms of what has been done well and where measurable targets and objectives have been met or exceeded.
4 Constructive criticism on areas where there is a need for improvement, offering support and advice as to how this could be achieved.
5 Listening to the appraisee's perspective, support requirements and needs together with their career aspirations.
6 Agreement on and recording of future targets and objectives, and what needs to be done to improve performance.

Many organizations have developed forms for taking staff through the appraisal system, covering achievement of objectives/targets, levels of competence for the role, training and development requirements and agreed actions.

There are a number of benefits to be gained from conducting a performance appraisal. These include a focus on improving performance, the gaining of useful two-way information, promotion of trust, collaboration on goal-setting and determining training requirements. On the other hand, performance appraisals are viewed by some as unnecessary if businesses already have a total quality management system in place. They are sometimes viewed as negative experiences and can lead to inflated ratings, as well as legal action if not carried out properly.

In carrying out a performance appraisal, the people manager needs to be honest, clear and specific, to give praise as well as criticism and to be sensitive to how his or her messages are likely to be received by those being appraised.

360-degree feedback

Another form of staff performance appraisal is 360-degree feedback, which collects views and feedback on an individual's performance from a range of people with whom the individual interacts on a day-to-day basis. It is claimed that this method provides a more rounded, accurate and less prejudiced view of the individual's performance. Normally, the views of between eight and ten people are sought through the use of questionnaires. These include customers as well as internal staff. The questionnaires include a series of statements which are rated on a scale, usually one to five. The feedback should be anonymized and conducted by someone skilled in the process.

Learning and development

Businesses that are concerned to develop their people and establish learning cultures are those which are more likely to be successful. It is beneficial for every team member to have a personal development plan (PDP) which sets out a list of time-bound actions to develop their knowledge and skills in the job as well as developing their competencies for career progression or specialism. Although the focus of PDPs is on the individual, the aim should be closely related to developing organizational capability.

Objectives, performance standards and measurement

The individual team member's objectives or targets should relate to a work plan similar to the one illustrated at the beginning of this chapter. They can be either results-orientated, relate to personal development objectives or both. Objectives and targets should be clearly defined and measurable, and agreed with the person concerned.

The benefits of good performance management

There are many benefits to be accrued from effective performance management at organizational, divisional and team levels. A transparent, challenging but achievable set of performance measures communicated effectively to a valued and involved workforce results in sound management control that is likely to lead to increased outputs/sales, improved delivery times, cost reductions, projects delivered on time and to budget, and the meeting of top-level strategic goals.

Summary

Performance management is a key part of the people manager's job. It involves having the right people and processes in place as both are fundamental to achieving an organization's objectives. It should take place at all levels of the business, from director of board level down to individuals. The existence of effective processes enables the people manager to set out and monitor work processes against targets and goals, and behaviour and development expectations of team members in line with the business's wider strategic objectives.

Performance management is useful for identifying areas of poor performance and those areas where the development of staff is needed.

We have touched upon the importance of culture and leadership in order to improve or manage performance, pointing out that some organizations have embedded cultures of continual performance improvement, while in others there is a reliance on systems and processes.

The benefits of good performance management were highlighted.

SUNDAY
MONDAY
TUESDAY
WEDNESDAY
THURSDAY
FRIDAY
SATURDAY

Fact-check (answers at the back)

1. Performance management takes place at:
   a) Organizational level ❏
   b) Team level ❏
   c) Individual level ❏
   d) All levels ❏

2. A team plan is used for:
   a) Setting strategic goals ❏
   b) Personal development ❏
   c) Performance management ❏
   d) Monitoring profit levels ❏

3. An organizational culture relates to:
   a) The industry sector ❏
   b) Management style ❏
   c) Country links ❏
   d) Values, beliefs and behaviours of an organization ❏

4. The performance management process involves:
   a) Leadership ❏
   b) Sales ❏
   c) Project management ❏
   d) Environmental management ❏

5. A performance management tool is:
   a) A workshop ❏
   b) 360-degree feedback ❏
   c) Critical Path Analysis ❏
   d) EFQM ❏

6. Performance appraisals relate to:
   a) Management ❏
   b) The performance plan ❏
   c) The team ❏
   d) Individuals ❏

7. The benefits of performance appraisal are:
   a) Increase in sales ❏
   b) Quality management ❏
   c) Work control ❏
   d) Determination of development requirements ❏

8. 360-degree appraisals seek the views of:
   a) Subordinates ❏
   b) Management ❏
   c) Peers ❏
   d) A range of contacts ❏

9. A personal development plan:
   a) Lists job tasks ❏
   b) Includes strategic aims ❏
   c) Focuses on learning and development ❏
   d) Identifies required behaviours ❏

10. Benefits of good performance include:
    a) Cost reductions ❏
    b) New market entry ❏
    c) Setting of strategic goals ❏
    d) Increase in staff turnover ❏

SATURDAY

How people managers develop their teams

On our final day, we are going to cover ways in which people managers can develop their teams. Team development is a fundamental part of the people manager's role, but often the most neglected due to pressure to meet work targets or personal ambitions.

However, there are obvious advantages to the people manager if he or she focuses on bringing together a cohesive, motivated and committed team. Such teams generally produce good quality work first time around, work tirelessly to achieve targets, come up with ideas and embrace change. They are also likely to have a low staff turnover and low sickness absenteeism.

We are going to explore the usefulness of a well-known group development model and the various ways in which team members can be developed. By the end of today you will have an appreciation of:

The importance of training and development

A well-known group development model

The various ways of training and developing staff

Building successful teams

Building a successful team is another major challenge faced by people managers. Work teams bring together groups of people with different personal characteristics, backgrounds and life experiences. Furthermore, the individuals are likely to have differing abilities and capacities for the tasks they are expected carry out. A people manager may either inherit a team that has been in existence for some time, be expected to bring together a new team, introduce new team members or drive forward change within the team. In each of these cases, team members need to learn to work together to function at maximum performance levels. It is the people manager's role to facilitate and encourage the efficient and effective functioning of the team.

The group development model

Almost half a century ago, Bruce Tuckman put forward a model of group development that comprises the stages of forming, storming, norming and performing. It is useful for the people manager to know about this model to develop an appreciation of group dynamics and their role in ensuring that the team works to maximum effect. It can also be helpful for the people manager to share their knowledge of the model with the team so that they can also understand the dynamics of the process.

The first stage of team development involves the initial forming of the team and can take place when a new team is set up or someone new joins an already established team. In this situation, people generally display their best behaviour because they are keen to be accepted and fit into the group. Every effort is made to avoid any conflict or disagreement by not dealing with any issues that may need to be addressed and ignoring any feelings that may arise. During this phase people tend to be more concerned about routine processes and procedures than outputs, while spending time gathering views and impressions of the other members of the team.

In the forming period, the people manager needs to support the team or new team member(s) in learning about the challenges and opportunities they face. Agreement also needs to be reached on team and/or individual goals and objectives prior to working on the tasks. Often there is a need for the people manager to adopt a directive management style during this phase, which gives him or her an opportunity to assess how the team members work individually and together and their responses in particular situations, such as those that are stressful.

The forming stage is followed by the storming stage where people open up and the contentious issues and disagreements avoided during the first stage are brought out into the open. It is a stage during which there is competition between different ideas and views that need to be reconciled. Some team members will find this phase particularly hard and try to evade addressing any disagreements by focusing on detailed, inconsequential tasks. This is a particularly difficult stage for the people manager because it is one of confronting issues, which inevitably gives rise to conflict. It is also the phase when team members make up their minds about the sort of management style that will be acceptable to them. The people manager will need to exercise tolerance and patience during this period, which is important if the team is to develop into an effective unit. He or she will probably need to continue with a directive management style, but be more available to team members to ensure sound decisions are made and professional behavioural standards upheld. It will also be important to be non-judgemental during this time and encourage individuals to accept their differences.

The norming stage is when the team's plans and goals have been agreed and accepted, and individuals settle down to take responsibility and carry out their particular tasks in pursuit of successful achievement of the team's goals. This is an easier stage for the people manager to handle and will require a more permissive management style.

The final stage is that of performing, which occurs when the team operates smoothly and functions efficiently and effectively. During this stage team members are highly motivated, skilled and knowledgeable, and are able to resolve any differences that may arise. The people manager's style in this phase should primarily be permissive.

Developing team members

One of the main functions of a people manager is the training and development of staff to grow a high-performing team that is making a valuable contribution to the achievement of organizational goals and targets. In developing staff, people managers need to take account of individual learning styles and decide on the most appropriate means of development for the individual and the team. It is important, therefore, to have an appreciation of learning styles and the main means of developing teams. These aspects are discussed below.

Learning styles

People have different ways of learning and these rarely vary throughout their working lives, so it is important for people managers to understand the various learning styles of the staff for whom they are responsible. People handle information in different ways. For example, some like information provided in a formal, structured way, some prefer to have a degree of independence in collecting and analysing information, while others enjoy processing complex information and developing theories. Some people, particularly extroverts, need a high level of involvement and participation in gathering and learning new information and theories. The majority of people have a dominant learning style or technique, but generally they have a mix of styles that they adapt for different circumstances.

Knowledge of your own learning style and those of the people you manage will help in the design of the most appropriate learning methods for individuals. The most commonly mentioned styles are the following.

- Visual learners learn through seeing and watching others, and respond best to pictures, diagrams, videos etc.
- Auditory learners learn through lectures, presentations and discussions with others. They prefer to talk things through and listen to others' views.

- Linguistic or verbal learners gain knowledge primarily through reading and writing or through listening to information.
- Physical or kinaesthetic people learn best through a hands-on approach and active exploration.
- Logical people learn through analysis, reasoning and logic.
- Social or interpersonal learners learn most effectively in groups or through interactions with other people.
- Solitary or intrapersonal learners work things through on their own through self-study.

The people manager has a number of methods available to him or her for training and developing staff to achieve a high-performing team. The main methods include on-the-job training, coaching, mentoring and formal training and education.

On-the-job training

On-the-job training, which involves staff being trained while remaining in the workplace, is considered to be one of the most effective means of training. It takes place in the normal working environment and can involve an experienced member of staff or the people manager working alongside a new staff member to pass on their knowledge and skills. The people manager has a valuable role in providing this training by selecting the most appropriate form of on-the-job training for the individual, or possibly delivering the training himself or herself. He or she should check that the staff member has received sufficient training to carry out the required tasks.

The most popular methods of on-the-job training include:

- demonstration or the use of instructions
- following manuals or operating procedures
- coaching, which is referred to in more detail below
- hands-on practice under supervision.

The advantages of on-the-job training are its cost-effectiveness and the fact that an employee is also productive while undergoing the training. Disadvantages are the possibility of disruption to work flow and the effectiveness of the training being dependent to a degree on the quality of the trainer.

Coaching

In recent years there has been a significant interest and growth in coaching as a means of developing staff and teams. Coaching is about helping to identify people's skills and capabilities and enabling them to use these to the best of their ability. Coaching in the workplace involves the individual being supported in learning to achieve a result or goal, or for personal or professional development purposes. Coaching may be done with individuals or with groups, either in person, over the phone or through online contact. Generally, it takes place for a limited amount of time.

Many organizations now expect people managers to coach their teams to achieve higher performance levels, personal growth and career development. As a people manager there is, therefore, merit in you developing the basic skills of coaching to improve your management and leadership abilities, and to be more effective in facilitating team meetings.

There are a number of models and styles of coaching; the most common involves asking questions and challenging the coachee to find the answers himself or herself. Coaches may also use inquiry, reflection and discussion to help those being coached to identify personal or business goals and develop action plans to achieve them. These goals may be many and varied, such as handling interpersonal relationships, improving behaviours, dealing with conflict or developing competence in particular areas.

Mentoring

Although there are close similarities between coaching and mentoring, and a coach can act as a mentor, there are differences between the two concepts. Mentoring involves a developmental relationship between an experienced individual and someone less experienced who would gain from the interactions between them. It uses the same models as coaching and demands the same skills, such as listening, questioning, clarifying and reframing. Mentoring is generally a longer-term relationship than coaching. It provides a learning opportunity for both parties.

As a people manager you are expected to act as a mentor to your staff. This is one of a number of ways in which you can help their development and improve their and the team's performance. Mentoring is an effective way of achieving higher productivity and growth. Generally, people value the opportunity to learn from others who are more experienced than them and those that actively seek mentoring are more likely to be successful. A mentor shares his or her own experiences with the mentee so that he or she can benefit from this in pursuit of his or her personal development. The aim is to share experience, encourage and ask pertinent questions in order to get mentees to learn for themselves. Showing interest in the person as well as the particular issue should form a part of the mentoring process. It is about listening and helping them rationalize their plans and can involve delivering unpopular messages that the mentee may not want to hear. Mentors transfer their knowledge and experience to others and do this willingly.

Apart from your role as a mentor to your staff, there would be value in selecting a mentor for yourself in order to have external, objective support in becoming a successful people manager.

Training and educational courses

There are usually costs associated with training and educational courses; the costs of the course itself and the costs to the business of not having a productive member for staff available for the course time. As a people manager you need to be certain that the training or educational course is in the organization's interest and that the contents of the proposed course cannot be delivered in a different and more cost-effective way. You also need to be certain that you have the budget to cover the costs and that other necessary team training will not suffer as a result. It might be worthwhile sending one team member on a course with the aim of them passing on their learning to others in the team.

There are several other ways in which a people manager can develop staff. These include secondment to another team or department, work shadowing, project work and job rotation. As a people manager, it is a prime task of yours to focus on the training and development of staff in order that the team can produce the best work possible in terms of quality and output. Identifying the need for training and development can be achieved through day-to-day observation or the performance management tools that were discussed on Friday. Once the need has been identified it is important to consider the most appropriate means of delivery of the training or development. This should be in accordance with the nature of the training or development required, the learning styles of the individual concerned and the team's overall budgetary and time constraints.

Summary

Finally, we have discussed the importance of people managers developing their teams and the various ways in which this can be done. The need to recognize and take account of differing skills levels and learning styles was stressed.

The well-known Tuckman group development model was explained, in particular the various stages of forming, storming and norming.

It was pointed out that the people manager should have knowledge of various learning styles so that he or she can assess the best way to develop individuals according to their preferred learning method.

A number of training and development methods were outlined, such as on-the-job training, coaching, mentoring, and training and educational courses.

SUNDAY

MONDAY

TUESDAY

WEDNESDAY

THURSDAY

FRIDAY

SATURDAY

Fact-check (answers at the back)

1. Which stage is not included in Tuckman's model?
a) Norming ☐
b) Performing ☐
c) Reforming ☐
d) Storming ☐

2. Conflict and disagreement emerges in which stage?
a) Performing ☐
b) Reforming ☐
c) Norming ☐
d) Storming ☐

3. A directive management style is suitable for which stage?
a) Performing ☐
b) Norming ☐
c) Storming ☐
d) Forming ☐

4. Which management style is appropriate for the performing stage?
a) Permissive ☐
b) Autocratic ☐
c) Bureaucratic ☐
d) Directive ☐

5. Which is not a recognized learning style?
a) Visual ☐
b) Coaching ☐
c) Physical ☐
d) Solitary ☐

6. On-the-job training does not involve:
a) Mentoring ☐
b) Coaching ☐
c) Educational courses ☐
d) Guidance ☐

7. Logical people learn through:
a) Interactions ☐
b) Seeing ☐
c) Discussions ☐
d) Reasoning ☐

8. Social people learn best:
a) Through analysis ☐
b) Lectures ☐
c) In groups ☐
d) Practical exploration ☐

9. On-the-job training involves:
a) Lectures ☐
b) Self-study ☐
c) Mentoring ☐
d) Group discussions ☐

10. Mentoring differs from coaching by:
a) Being longer term ☐
b) Questioning ☐
c) Reflecting ☐
d) Challenging ☐

Surviving in tough times

The world of work is subject to rapid change and there is now little job security for people managers or others, regardless of whether you are employed in the public, private or voluntary sector. In order to survive, you have to be adaptable, flexible and demonstrate your ability to continually develop new skills. The environment within which people managers work is often highly competitive and demanding. There are pressures on all organizations to reduce costs while also being expected to deliver more. This can lead to significant stress. The following advice is provided to support you in surviving during tough times.

1 Demonstrate that you are indispensable

If cuts in staffing are taking place in a business, senior managers will be reluctant to make redundant those people managers who have demonstrated their value to the company or organization. While it is true that no one is indispensable, if you have shown exceptional commitment by going beyond your duties on a number of occasions, the likelihood is that management will do what they can to retain your services in times of cut-backs because of your value to the business.

2 Be your own PR (public relations)

You may be an excellent people manager and extremely valuable to the organization, but if senior management are unaware of your successes they are unlikely to consider you for retention if times are tough. In order to secure your continued employment and possibly obtain advancement, it is vital that you let those in positions of authority and influence know what you are achieving and your value to the business. Wide communication about your own and your team's successes and business improvement ideas can help in this respect. Engaging in informal discussions in the coffee bar or after meetings is a subtle way of getting the message across that you are highly committed to the future of the business.

3 Be aware of organizational politics

Organizational politics are difficult to avoid. It is a sad fact of life that in the majority of organizations many people are more concerned about playing organizational politics in order to pursue their own career advancement than the welfare of those for whom they are responsible and the performance of the business. Survival in tough times means being aware of organizational politics and the behaviours of the key actors, and playing a part in the politics to ensure you are not overlooked or being subjected to reputational damage as during difficult times the worst of human behaviours can emerge.

4 Demonstrate flexibility and adaptability

Those employees who have demonstrated a great deal of flexibility and adaptability in carrying out their jobs are more likely to be retained during company restructuring or downsizing exercises. In both these situations, job roles are likely to be changed so if you have shown rigidity in your tasks and a reluctance to do things differently, senior management would be less inclined to find you a position in a newly formed or restructured business.

5 Save or make money for the company

All organizations are having to reduce costs and increase profits in order to survive. If you can show that you have saved money through reducing wastage, cutting down on travel expenses, using staff resources efficiently and streamlining processes, you are more likely to survive in the organization during difficult times. It would also be to your advantage if you could come up with some worthy new service delivery or new product ideas that have the potential to increase the business's profits.

6 Monitor trends and act upon them

There are so many business failures as a result of not keeping up with and adapting to economic, social and environmental trends. We operate today in a global economy and within a fast, unpredictable environment. The survival of businesses is dependent on keeping up with economic, social and environmental changes, in particular those that affect a business's customers or clients. These changes also present opportunities for innovation or diversification. Although, strictly, this is the role of more senior managers and directors, people managers who can contribute to internal discussions around the future of the business by presenting a wider, strategic perspective are going to be looked upon favourably in terms of retention and/or promotion.

7 Keep your CV updated

It is too easy to neglect keeping your CV updated. We are all busy people and while in employment do not always see the need to maintain our CVs. However, if your CV or career summary is not regularly updated you will soon forget some significant achievements that could impress a future employer. In tough times, it is worth reviewing your CV monthly and comparing it with job advertisements to identify knowledge and skill areas for development, and to act upon these.

8 Develop and widen your transferable skills

It is worthwhile monitoring the job market to see what opportunities are available and the types of knowledge, skills and experience companies and other organizations are seeking. This information should be used to develop your transferable people management skills in a way that will be attractive to a number of organizations in a variety of sectors. The principles of people management and the tasks involved in successfully managing people are the same regardless of the type of business. However, it is vital that you have a number of examples of the sort of experience and skills deployment future employers are likely to be seeking. It is your responsibility to seek out this experience and develop the skills demanded by future potential employers.

9 Never stop learning

Current and future employers welcome people managers who are shown to be keen on their own personal development. In people management you never stop learning. Every situation and the people involved are different and require a different way of managing. A focus on your own continual professional development, particularly through reflection and mentoring, while keeping up with wider professional developments is beneficial for you, your team and your organization. It also helps you stand out as exceptionally committed in tough times.

10 Network and maintain good relationships

Generally, people choose to do business and work with people they like and respect. Business-related relationships within and outside the organization are therefore important. These relationships need to be maintained and developed as there is no way of knowing when you may need the help and support of a business colleague, especially during difficult times. Always be pleasant and helpful to people you interact with in a work context and where possible do favours. In all probability this will be repaid to you in tougher times. Networking continually within and outside the organization is vital if you are to survive as a successful people manager in difficult and challenging times. If you are not always in view, people will forget you or be under the impression that you are content in a secure job.

Answers

Sunday: 1c; 2d; 3a; 4a; 5c; 6c; 7d; 8d; 9c; 10d.

Monday: 1c; 2c; 3a; 4 Specific, Measurable, Attainable, Relevant, Time-bound; 5b; 6d; 7c; 8d; 9d; 10c.

Tuesday: 1d; 2c; 3c; 4a; 5a; 6c; 7c; 8d; 9b; 10d.

Wednesday: 1d; 2c; 3c; 4b; 5c; 6b; 7b; 8a; 9b; 10c.

Thursday: 1c; 2b; 3b; 4a; 5c; 6 Political, Economic, Social, Technological; 7c; 8d; 9b; 10c.

Friday: 1d; 2c; 3d; 4a; 5b; 6b; 7d; 8d; 9c; 10a.

Saturday: 1c; 2d; 3d; 4a; 5b; 6c; 7d; 8c; 9b; 10a.

ALSO AVAILABLE IN THE 'IN A WEEK' SERIES

BODY LANGUAGE FOR MANAGEMENT • BOOKKEEPING AND ACCOUNTING • CUSTOMER CARE • DEALING WITH DIFFICULT PEOPLE • EMOTIONAL INTELLIGENCE • FINANCE FOR NON-FINANCIAL MANAGERS • INTRODUCING MANAGEMENT • MANAGING YOUR BOSS • MARKET RESEARCH • NEURO-LINGUISTIC PROGRAMMING • OUTSTANDING CREATIVITY • PLANNING YOUR CAREER • SPEED READING • SUCCEEDING AT INTERVIEWS • SUCCESSFUL APPRAISALS • SUCCESSFUL ASSERTIVENESS • SUCCESSFUL BUSINESS PLANS • SUCCESSFUL CHANGE MANAGEMENT • SUCCESSFUL COACHING • SUCCESSFUL COPYWRITING • SUCCESSFUL CVS • SUCCESSFUL INTERVIEWING

For information about other titles in the series, please visit www.inaweek.co.uk